THROUGH

BRANDON MAURIZIO

ISBN 978-1-0980-7608-5 (paperback)
ISBN 978-1-0980-9288-7 (hardcover)
ISBN 978-1-0980-7609-2 (digital)

Christian Faith Publishing, Inc.
832 Park Avenue
Meadville, PA 16335
www.christianfaithpublishing.com

Printed in the United States of America

INTRODUCTION

This can't be real life, can it? Surely, this is just a nightmare that I can't wake up from. The air conditioning is blasting down on the top of my head. I know I should be cold, but I can't feel a thing. I look to my left and see the love of my life hooked up to a machine in one arm, while the other arm is covered in bracelets that identify her blood type. I look to my right and see the names of nurses who I've never met scribbled illegibly on a dry erase board that seems to be rarely cleaned. Time has slowed down to a torturous rate tonight. I am too tired to cry. None of this feels real. Our nurse would come in on occasion, asking if we needed anything. Coffee? Food? There's no time to eat, and ironically, too much time all simultaneously. Looking back, I'm sure we did need something, but I was too numb to know. Every time the doctor or nurse entered our room, there was a somber wind that followed them. It's like knowing that someone knows something about you that you don't want anyone knowing, you know? My bed for the night was a cold, stale leathery chair that creaked loudly every time you shifted ever so slightly. Whenever I tried to relax and lean into it, that shattering squeak reminded me that there's no possible way to relax right now. I tried to get my mind off what was happening by turning on the TV. The picture was faded, and it sounded as if it were coming from underwater. It was just reruns anyways. Who was I kidding? Nothing was going to make this better. Nothing was going to stop the pain. Every five minutes, I would look up at the clock on the wall feeling as though an hour had passed. This was an experience I would never wish upon anyone, even my enemies. The pain was unexplainable. My eyes burned from exhaustion. I wanted to cry, but the tears wouldn't come. So many questions bombarded my mind. Why is this happening? Why me? After all I've done for You, God, why me? What's the point of praying when things like this are still going to happen? God, if you're real, if you love us, make this stop. Make the pain go away. Thoughts of what could have been, like playing at the park with him, hearing him say his first words, watching him ride his bike for the first time with no training wheels, meeting his first girlfriend, teaching him to love and appreciate God's Word—all those dreams gone in the blink of an eye. If I'm being completely honest, I felt as though that night was never going to end. No amount of support could have made me feel less alone. Could I have done anything differently to prevent this from happening? Was it my fault?

This day was the first day of the worst year of my life. The year 2019, undoubtedly and unrivaled, will be forever etched into my memory as the year that I wish never happened. You might be thinking, "Brandon, you're a pastor! You know that God causes all things to work together for the good of those who are called according to His purposes and who love Him! You know you need to trust in Him with all your heart and leaneth noteth on your own understanding. YOU KNOW HE HAS PLANS FOR YOU, plans to give you hope and a future. You know that God is close to the brokenhearted." Look, I believe ALL of that to be true. I believe that with my whole heart, but if I'm being completely honest, there are experiences in life, seemingly impossible-to-go-through experiences, that I wish I could just skip over or avoid altogether. We all do, right? If you say that you don't, I'll introduce you to my holy advice-giving neighbors, and they'll teach you how to tell the truth. Don't test me. I'll do it. Humans today aren't good at feeling pain. I mean, who wants to be good at feeling pain? Our culture distracts, self-medicates, and does just about anything to avoid confronting hurt. But here's the truth: the healing process doesn't begin until we allow ourselves to be broken. This book was birthed out of pure brokenness. Subconsciously, I think I used to consider myself a professional at avoiding pain, until the weight of that pain was too heavy to carry and too dark to hide from.

Through is a book all about life, really. Celebrating the good times, acknowledging the bad. Embracing the easy times and persisting through the not-so-easy times. It's about reminding you that your story has just begun. It's about infusing faith and hope into the most hopeless of situations. This book has been resonating in my heart for a long time now. Believe me, it has taken a lot to actually discipline myself to sit down and write out my thoughts. I'm not a professional writer, by all means, but I really do pray that the words in this book resonate deeply within you. That the illustrations and stories are relatable to you. That at the end of it, you feel encouraged knowing that you're not alone. That you feel inspired to take steps forward in your life. That you gain a new sense of purpose in the pain. That you truly begin to believe that the mess you're in right now will one day be transformed into a message. That nothing is EVER wasted. That no matter how tempted you are to give up, or how desperately you desire to avoid the challenge you're faced with, you won't. You'll confront that bad boy head-on. Why? Because you are stronger than you give yourself credit for.

Throughout the pages and chapters of this book, I'll share with you what I've discovered and learned from walking through what literally felt like a never-ending horror story. I'll let you in on personal things that not a lot of people know about in the hopes that it speaks to your heart and that you feel a sense of relatability. There's something about knowing that someone has been through the place that you're in right now that sparks a sense of hope. You deserve hope.

I want to tell you, candidly so, there is no way I could have ever imagined making it through any of this without the constant love, encouragement, and support of my wife, Karen. You're truly a gift to me. Your strength and unwavering faith in God, no matter the circumstance, will always inspire me. I love you more than words can say. You're my best friend, my partner, the love of my life, and simply put, you're just really freakin' cool. I want to be cool like you.

Above all, this book wouldn't be possible if it weren't for the unfailing, unconditional, mind-blowing, life-changing, wall-breaking love of Jesus Christ. Without Your promises, which are truly an anchor for our souls, and Your sweet presence, there's no way I would be here sharing this today. Thank You for giving Your life so I could live. Thank You for enduring THROUGH the cross so we can have a relationship today. You're my everything.

To you reading this, my friend, though we may have never met, I want this to feel like we are sitting down at Starbucks together sharing a conversation over some epic beverages and pastries. I want it to feel like a big ol' bear hug. I want it to be like wrapping yourself in a fluffy blanket that you just pulled out from the dryer. I want it to be like the motivational speech Yoda gives to Luke on the planet of Dagobah when Luke is about to give up on his Jedi training. I want it to be an outstretched hand to help you up if you feel as though you've fallen. Ultimately, I want this to feel like the encouraging words from someone who has perhaps felt something similar to what you're feeling right now.

There could be a couple reasons as to why this book is currently in your hands. You have this book right now because someone believed it would help you through a very challenging situation, you're wanting to help someone through a challenging situation and you want a fresh perspective as to how, or you're just looking for an easy read. Either way, the things you'll read in the pages to come will help you now in life or, I guarantee it, help you through something that seems unbearable that will come someday. Life is unpredictable, confusing at times, and sometimes, let's be honest, straight up hard. No matter how difficult the trial may be, no matter how badly you want to ignore it or avoid it, it's time to confront it and walk through it. I promise, you'll be stronger on the other side. You're tougher than you give yourself credit for. You're more than a conqueror. You're an overcomer! Let's pick you up, dust off those knees of yours, and slowly take one step forward. It's time to start going through.

1

FAST-FORWARD

Jack Bauer is one of my heroes (after Jesus, of course). Don't judge me. Hands down, bar-none one of the most hardcore humans to ever walk the planet. If he and Chuck Norris had an arm wrestling contest, I think Chuck Norris would have at least had a bit of a struggle. Dare I say even break a sweat. (Let's be honest, Chuck Norris doesn't lose anything). Just in case the name Jack Bauer doesn't send chills down your spine like it does mine, let me introduce you to him. He's the main character of one of the greatest action TV shows of all time, *24*. The entire season takes place over a twenty-four-hour period (hence the name) and is all about how Jack Bauer saves the world from eminent destruction. I never could figure out how they went an entire twenty-four hours with no food or bathroom breaks. Oh well. I guess Jack Bauer was too hardcore to pee. My fondest memories of this show surround not only the show but the process of going over to my friend Tyler's house to watch the show on Monday nights with his mom. Now before you start questioning the fact that I watched the show with only his mom and not him, no one else was into the show like Elayne and I were. We always gave the others the opportunity to watch the show with us, of course. Just no one really cared. Their loss! Every Monday night, when I went over to partake in the *24* ritual, Elayne always had fresh sweet tea brewed up to perfection and a life-changing, heart-melting, cavity-inducing homemade caramel popcorn. Though I've tried to make the recipe on multiple

7

accounts, nothing ever came close to the caliber of Elayne's caramel corn. Something about the combination of sweet tea and caramel corn that warms my heart even to this day. I'd walk through the door, and she'd have tea and corn ready to go. As soon as we settled in, I remember her voice always saying, "B, are you ready to see how Jack (we were on a first-name basis) saves the world tonight?" Boy, was I ready. Every week. Rain or shine. Jack, let's do this.

Elayne and her husband, Kenny, are some of the sweetest, loving, most encouraging people (outside family) that I have ever known. While Elayne homeschooled her kids, Kenny had his own drywall business, which would keep him busy. No one told stories quite like Kenny did. His soft Southern accent recalled life experiences in such vivid detail that it made you feel as though you were actually there with him. He had a story to compliment just about any topic that came up. Elayne loved many things, but she loved three things in particular: Jesus, history, and baseball. In fact, she loved baseball so much that she even gave her daughter the initials of MLB. Amazing. On top of raising two kids and working full-time, they both pastored a local church called Destiny Christian Center. This church was the church that I met Jesus in when I was fifteen. They took the time to explain, in simplicity, the life-changing message of God's love and grace. They sat down for countless hours with this skinny punk rock kid with earrings, lip piercings, ripped-up checkered Vans slip-ons, and tight jeans and just invested. No matter how rough I was on the outside, Kenny and Elayne took me in as one of their own. That investment changed my life.

Those Monday night *24* sessions are such a huge component as to who I am today. I would get there early, not only for the popcorn and sweet tea but to ask Kenny and Elayne questions about the Bible and about life. Everyone needs a Kenny and Elayne. There were times that we got into such deep conversations regarding a particular topic that it would bleed into the time when mine and Elayne's show would start. I'll never forget the first time our conversation was getting close to the starting of *24*. I had this intuition that knew Jack Bauer was about to come on the TV. I think Elayne was able to sense my shiftiness because, without me even saying a word, she said, "B, it's okay. We have DVR." DVR? I've never heard of this sorcery. Will it transport Jack to our living room? Friends, let me tell you, DVR changed me. It's a luxury that you'd expect someone with heated toilet seats to have in their home, yet humble Kenny and Elayne were sitting on this magical device. Get this, it would RECORD LIVE TELEVISION. That's right. You read correctly. RECORD LIVE TELEVISION. Most of the time, if we didn't get into a deep conversation about the Bible, we would strategically wait a bit before starting our *24*-athon. Why, you may ask? To fast forward through the commercials, of course. People used DVR to record shows that they were going to miss, but in my opinion, the best feature of DVR is being able to skip commercials. Now the invention of the light bulb was a pretty important thing if you ask me, but in an extremely close second is DVR. Do you enjoy commercials? Are you the type of person that watches the Super Bowl solely for the commercials? NOPE. Commercials really irritate me. That's not the reason I'm on this channel. Give me Jack Bauer! I don't care about deals that Jack in the Box are making available at one in the morning. Give me the other Jack! I don't need to hear the long list of awful side effects a migraine medicine creates. Please, just resume the show. I'll never forget the first time I realized that Elayne had DVR. We were watching *24*, and when it came time for the commercial, she busted out her remote and fast-forwarded right on through it. I was shocked. Simply shocked. HOW DID YOU DO THAT?! Three magical letters: DVR. Welcome to the future.

There are times, if I am being completely honest, that I wish real life had DVR. Right? There are certain experiences that I wish I could just fast-forward through or, while we're at it, avoid altogether. There are times in life when I wish I had a remote control like Adam Sandler did in that one movie that I can't remember the name of. You know, the one where he controlled time with a remote? Yeah, I wish I had one of those bad boys. I'd love to hit rewind once in a while. Wouldn't that be nice? Having the ability to go back and change the things in life that didn't really work out the way you wanted them to, or maybe you made a horrible decision last night that you wish never happened. Wouldn't it be great to just hit rewind and prevent it from ever happening? Have you ever said something to someone that, at the very moment it left your mouth, you wish you never said? Rewind would be SO nice. That happens to me all the time with Karen. Or what about a pause button? Mmm, pause button. Have you ever been so busy and stressed out that the only time you stop going crazy is the moment your head hits your pillow? Maybe even then it takes a while for you to fall asleep because your mind won't stop. It would be so great to just hit the pause button in the times when you have a project due or a test to study for also, right? Just a little more time. Or maybe you're having a blast at Disneyland with your family and never want it to stop. It would be amazing to hit the pause button and stay in that moment forever. Life really does go by so fast when you think about it. The rewind button and pause button are cool and all, but how nice would a fast forward be though? Imagine this: in the times when you feel like life is unbearably challenging, in the moments when you are being stretched beyond your limit, in the moments when you just want to give up and hit eject, it would be so amazing to just fast-forward through them. Or maybe, like a DVD, skip the chapter altogether. Here's the truth though, life isn't like that. Life isn't like that AT ALL. Life is full of hardships. Life is full of brokenness, sorrows, and wrecks. Life is full of times that are anything but enjoyable. You might even be in one of those seasons right now. A season that you wish you could skip or pause or fast-forward through. Wouldn't that be nice? But here's the reality. Life keeps moving forward. Time keeps ticking on. Hardships happen to everyone, and until we make the decision to move through them, we will never heal, we will never discover purpose, and life will gradually become this bland thing we survive rather than a beautiful adventure in which we thrive. Going through things is scary, unpredictable, and sometimes seemingly unbearable. If that's how you're feeling right now, I want you to know you're not alone. In fact, even from the beginning of creation, there have been instances of people going through challenging things.

The Bible is a book that's all about humans going through difficult things. Even while going through hardships, God was present with them when they did. Literally from the very beginning, this was the cycle. God hooked up Adam and Eve, the first humans, with a perfect paradise to live in called the garden of Eden. The way the Bible describes Eden is simply breathtaking. There were rivers with gold in them, there was every single animal on earth there with them, and did I mention that they were naked? How cool would it be to not have to worry about wearing clothes, right? God gave them free reign to do anything they wanted anywhere they wanted, except for this one single tree that they needed to stay away from. They could eat fruit from any tree in the entire garden except for this one tree. "Why would God put something in the Garden of Eden that they couldn't have?" you may be asking yourself. Well, you see, the reason why God created us in the first place was to have a genuine relationship with us. He loves us beyond what words can encapsulate, and He desires for us to love Him back. True love is a choice, and God wanted to create us with free will to give us the choice to love Him back. If He forced us to love Him like a puppet or robot, that wouldn't at all be genuine love. The tree was simply present there to be a choice. Choose to obey God's Word, and by doing so, choose to love and respect God. Like classic humans though, Adam and Eve messed up. They took a big ol' bite out of the only thing they weren't supposed to and, as a result, invited sin, brokenness, and separation from God into existence. Sin separates us from God. I'm not sure what comes to your mind when you think of the word *sin*. Maybe you think of stealing or murdering or looking at things you're not supposed to. Maybe you think of getting wasted or doing drugs. Sin, by definition, is simply missing the mark, anything less than perfection. Think of it like archery. (Sidenote: I tried archery in the mountains of Colorado one time, and it was REALLY challenging). In archery, anything that's not a bull's-eye, a perfect shot, is considered sin. The Bible says that the consequence of sin is death. Sin causes death. Sin SUCKS. I always say that sin takes you farther than you want to go, keeps you longer than you want to stay, and costs you more than you want to pay. Sin entered the world through Adam and Eve's disobedience to God in the garden of Eden, and because of that one act, humanity was now in this cycle of destruction, anger, hatred, and anything nasty you could think of. If you think that the Bible is boring, just read through the book of Genesis. There are some GNARLY stories. This is what happens because of sin. Sin causes brokenness. Sin causes people to do bad things to other people. Sin invites sickness, brokenness, and other side effects of death into existence. This wasn't part of God's original design. BUT GOD, in His INCREDIBLE grace, set motion to the rescue mission to top all rescue missions. Yes, even more epic than Jack Bauer. God literally put on flesh and bones and came to this world that He created. He did this because of one driving factor: love. In the Old Testament, the way people made payments for their sins, making themselves right with God, was through animal blood sacrifices (intense, right?). Because remember, the cost of sin is death. There needed to be atonement for the sins. If you want an interesting read, check out the book of Leviticus. Leviticus is a list of rules and regulations to purify the people of their sins so that they can worship God in His presence and experience relationship with Him. That is what it's all about after all, relationship. That's why God created us in the first place, for relationship. Because the whole animal sacrifice thing was only temporary, quick fixes, Jesus accomplished what the animal sacrifices couldn't. By giving His life as a sacrifice, His blood that was shed on the cross literally paid the price for our sins. God's wrath, justice, and anger because of sin was all taken out on Jesus when He was on the cross. He did what sacrificing Scruffy couldn't do. Rather than paraphrasing this concept, I'm going to add a portion of a book in the Bible called Hebrews to explain this idea more clearly:

> The old system under the law of Moses was only a shadow, a dim preview of the good things to come, not the good things themselves. The sacrifices under that system were repeated again and again, year after year, but they were never able to provide perfect cleansing for those who came to worship. If they could have provided perfect cleansing, the sacrifices would have stopped, for the worshipers would have been purified once for all time, and their feelings of guilt would have

disappeared. But instead, those sacrifices actually reminded them of their sins year after year. For it is not possible for the blood of bulls and goats to take away sins. That is why, when Christ came into the world, He said to God, "You did not want animal sacrifices or sin offerings. But you have given me a body to offer. You were not pleased with burnt offerings or other offerings for sin." Then I said, "Look, I have come to do your will, O God—as it is written about me in the Scriptures…" for God's will was for us to be made holy by the sacrifice of the body of Jesus Christ, once for all time. Under the old covenant, the priest stands and ministers before the altar day after day, offering the same sacrifices again and again, which can never take away sins. But our High Priest offered Himself to God as a single sacrifice for sins, good for all time. Then He sat down in the place of honor at God's right hand. There He waits until His enemies are humbled and made a footstool under His feet. For by that one offering He forever made perfect those who are being made holy. (Hebrews 10:1–7, 10–14)

How cool is that? Thank God we don't still need to do animal sacrifices, right? I really like my dogs. So with all that in mind NOW, all we need to do is believe it, receive it, and walk it out. When you receive what Jesus did for you, all your sins are completely forgiven—past, present, future. ALL sins forgiven. Because your sin is forgiven, you can stand boldly in relationship with the One who created you. God also knows everything about you. The Bible even says that He knows the number of hairs on your head! For people who don't have a bunch of hair (like me), that doesn't hit as hard, but it doesn't take away from how much He loves you! His thoughts toward you (which are all good, by the way) outnumber the grains of sand on earth. I challenge you to try and count grains of sand the next time you're at a beach of some sort. It will exhaust you and cause you to feel so loved all at the same time. If you're reading this and you feel like you've done something unforgivable, something that has disqualified you from receiving a kind of love like this, God's love goes beyond our understanding. Realizing that you can do nothing to make God love you less is a truth that propels us forward. It's THAT good.

Though we can have restored relationship with God because of what Jesus did on the cross, it doesn't mean we won't still go through hard times here on earth. If you believe that following Jesus is an instant end-all to problems, pain, and challenges, you are setting yourself up for disappointment. Maybe you've given the Jesus thing a try and you feel as though it didn't quite work out for you. Or maybe you had in your mind that if you opened up your heart to Jesus, attended church a couple times a month, prayed the prayers at the end of services, gave financially to a charity, and even memorized a song or two that they sang before the message, all your problems would magically go away. I have news for you, my friend: following Jesus doesn't make your problems go away. Sorry to burst your holy bubble. Saying yes to Him doesn't mean that there won't be challenges in life. If you've been told that the Bible promises us a trouble-free life, you've been lied to. On the contrary, Jesus promises us in John 16:33 that we will have MANY trials and sorrows. Check it out:

> I have told you these things, so that in Me you may have [perfect] peace. In the world YOU HAVE tribulation and distress and suffering, but be courageous [be confident, be undaunted, be filled with joy]; I have overcome the world. [My conquest is accomplished, My victory abiding.]"
> (John 16:33 AMP)

The word *tribulation* in this passage of scripture can mean many things. It can mean troubles, difficulties, problems, worries, anxieties, burdens, tragedies, sorrows, traumas, setbacks, etc. If you have the idea that nothing bad will ever happen to you, you have a false understanding of what being a Christ follower actually is. In fact, acknowledging the reality of challenges will help safeguard your overall enjoyment of life. This book is all about embracing that truth, learning what the Bible says about it, and boldly going through the trials when, not if, they come. Though at times you will want to approach your life like a good ol' DVR and fast-forward through the difficulties, you have to make the decision to face troubles and challenges head-on. You must, beforehand, make a choice to not attempt to fast-forward in fear, pause in exhaustion, or even eject and give up. You need to determine for yourself to slowly and intentionally make it through this one brave step at a time. It's not over for you. In fact, this is just the beginning of your story.

2

FILL THAT FLASK

Before diving any further into this book, I want to be completely honest and forthright with you. If you haven't noticed already, I use a ton of scriptures and stories from the Bible to illustrate points and ideas. I believe that the Bible is a collection of words that are straight from God's heart. I believe that it is designed to show us His character, bring clarity to what life is actually all about, and to be an instrument used to shape and form us into who we were created to be. Though it has been around for more than a couple thousand years, I think you'll be pleasantly surprised to see just how relevant it is to life as we know it today. The same issues that we go through on a heart level today are the same issues humans went through in Biblical times. Don't believe me? Buckle your seat belt, my friend. It's about to get real. I'm not sure what you personally believe about the Bible or what your experience with church has been, but since God and His Word have been such a source of strength, peace, and hope for me, it would be outright selfish of me to not share it with you. Strength, peace, and hope sound pretty amazing right about now, am I right? I challenge you to have an open mind, beyond any preconceived opinion you may already have developed about God. Try allowing the Scriptures to penetrate your heart and mind. Who knows? It might actually help!

In the Bible, there's a guy named Samuel. Samuel was pretty much a boss from the moment he was born. Long story short, before

16

he was born, his mom, Hannah, was having a really hard time conceiving. The Bible uses phrases like deep anguish, sorrow, and bitter crying to describe the emotions she expressed about not being able to get pregnant. Talk about going THROUGH something, right? There's one recorded instance when she was so expressive and emotionally distraught in how she was praying to God that a guy in the temple thought she was wasted. Have you ever been so discouraged, so fed up with your situation, that people around you thought that you were drunk? Beginning to see the Bible as relevant already? The guy that thought she had a little too much sippy-sip happened to be a prophet. Prophet is a fancy title given to someone who simply hears from God and delivers messages to people on His behalf. This prophet told her that God was going to grant her request, which, of course, brought some encouragement and hope to her heart. Sometime after that, Samuel's mom became pregnant with him and gave birth to him. His mom named him Samuel because Samuel sounds like the Hebrew term for "heard by God." Can I tell you right now that no matter how alone you feel, how dire your circumstances may look, how many sleepless nights you've had this week, how many tears have rolled down your cheek, how many people thought you were intoxicated because of how sad you were, God hears you. No matter how impossible a breakthrough seems to be, God not only hears you. He sees you and cares about you. Just because you're in the middle of something challenging doesn't mean that God isn't present. Did you know that the Bible talks more about God being present with people through their challenges than it does about God delivering them from their challenges?

After Samuel was born, his mom was so beyond thankful to God for granting her request that she offered Samuel back to God to serve Him in the place of worship, the very same place just three years prior where she was calling out to God in anguish. Sidenote: I've noticed that God will oftentimes allow us to go back to the very places of distress that He brought us through to give us the opportunity to worship Him with the things we acquired along the journey, things we would have never picked up if we wouldn't have ever been in the struggle in the first place. It's a beautiful cycle, really.

Samuel grew up in the tabernacle, serving under the same prophet that gave his mom the encouraging words before she got pregnant with him. Talk about a full circle, am I right? Samuel would only see his mom and dad once a year when they came back to offer their sacrifices to God. Think about that for a moment: Samuel lived his life day in day out completely immersed in and committed to learning, growing, and serving God. Though I'm sure Samuel picked up on a bunch of nifty tricks in his time at the tabernacle, there is one thing in particular that stands out to me when reading about Samuel—his unique opportunities to hear God's voice. I am a firm believer that God speaks to us today, just like we read about Him doing in the Bible. God speaks to everyone. Not just the religious folks, not just the pastors, preachers, or teachers. Not just the nuns, saints, and monks. God speaks to EVERYONE. God could even be speaking to you as you read these words right now. If you think that God's voice is BIG and BOOMING and sounds a little like Morgan Freeman, you might be missing out on actually hearing it. For a majority of my life growing up in church, I never understood the concept of hearing God's voice. I learned Sunday school songs about it, hand motions and all. I even watched *VeggieTales* cartoons about it. Even with all that experience, I still couldn't honestly say that I ever heard God speak to me. A vivid memory I have in regard to hearing God's voice, or a lack thereof if you had asked me at the moment, was up at a summer camp I attended when I was in the seventh grade. Before you jump to any conclusions about me being super spiritual and having my life together in junior high, let me stop you. I'm pretty sure I smelled like greasy pizza every day, wore puka shell necklaces way past the time they were in style, and rocked the icy tip spiked haircut. I was far from having my life figured out and even further away from being spiritually mature. I remember at this particular camp, the speaker was really adamant about the students hearing God's voice. Okay. I'll give it a shot. The human foosball at this camp was fun, and the chili cheese fries were, well, let's just say they didn't treat me well. But why not leave this camp having heard the voice of the Creator of heaven and earth? That is what the speaker presented it like. Following the session, he had every one of the students spread out on the campground, pull out their Bibles, and wait for God to speak to them. (As a youth pastor now, the thought of students spreading out over a campground wherever they want, with no designated oversight, sends chills down my spine.) After the session concluded, I wandered around for a while before coming across my spot. I saw this stump that was standing all alone, at just the right height for my skinny little legs to push myself up on. I dusted off the top of the stump, jumped up on it, busted out my "I'm a part of God's Army" Bible, opened it up to a random page, and sat there, waiting for God to speak to me. There's something about silence in the mountains that's deafening. I was expecting to hear an audible voice come forth, rattling the ground and shaking the trees. If not that, I mean maybe a dove was going to descend from heaven carrying a golden scroll with God's Word. Needless to say, I sat in silence, waiting for God to speak. One silent minute led to the next, and my confusion as a little junior high student grew. I thought that the passionate pastor guys said that God speaks to people? In all honesty, a word from God in that moment would have been really nice. That was, after all, the summer around the time when my parents separated. I closed my Bible, got up from my log of choice, dusted off my oversized cargo shorts, and continued on with my camp experience. Was it that God didn't speak to me, or did I simply not understand His voice?

Radios creep me out. They really do. The idea surrounding the concept of these radio waves that are invisible to the eye, floating around in the air, is a challenging one for me to grasp. When I was younger, I was passionate. I mean, PASSIONATE about listening to Radio Disney on AM 710. Every time we were in the car, no matter how long the trip was, I would request to hear my Radio Disney. I was passionate about it, until one day, without warning, AM 710 changed into a sports broadcasting channel. Ew. I would much rather listen to my Little Romeo than hearing about how the Dodgers were doing. This gives you yet another glimpse into the type of child I was. Radio waves travel through the air at the speed of light from a transmitter until it reaches something to receive it. The antenna on your car or those little silver antennas that you would extend on an old radio (I know, right?) are the receivers that would snatch these tiny radio waves zipping through the air. If I wanted to listen to my Radio Disney, I would tune my little radio receiver to AM 710, and it would pick up that specific wave. Just like how radio waves are always present, God too is always speaking. We don't hear the radio waves until we tune to the right channel. As cliché as this might sound, we don't hear God's voice until we—you guessed it—tune in to the right channel. A VITAL component to going through things is having a guide. God is our guide, and how He guides us is with His voice. Maybe rather than it being a super clear station, you've just heard static when talking to God. Maybe you believe that God only spoke to people in biblical times. Maybe you believe that God's too busy running the universe to take the time to speak to you. Or maybe God has been speaking to you your whole life, up to this very moment, but you haven't had anyone explain to you how to tune in to it.

I've noticed that God talks to different people in different ways. I'll give you some examples. To some, He speaks through nature. That sense of awe that fills your heart when you glimpse into a sunset that is breathtaking can be God speaking to you. When you have a sense of overwhelming peace that comes from taking a deep breath of fresh mountain air when you wake up early for a hike on a camping trip. If you've ever seen the Grand Canyon, it truly is grand. Seeing something so big can provoke us to think, *Wow! I'm seriously so small. God is so big. What do I really have to worry about?* Boom! God speaking. God can speak through music, conversations with people, pictures we see, words we read, and so much more. When you're reading the Bible and a word or phrase jumps out at you and pierces your heart, that can absolutely be God speaking to you. The question to ask when trying to figure out if it's God speaking to you (or if it's the burrito you ate for lunch) is "Does the Bible confirm this idea?" or "Would Jesus say this?" Hearing God's voice becomes way less complicated and way more encouraging when you begin to look at it through this lens. I'll give you a cool example of one of the first times I realized that God spoke to me. One evening, I decided to go on a walk. Quick sidenote: I love going on walks. They are way less stressful than going on runs. Runs remind me that I'm out of shape, and I don't like being reminded about being out of shape. This particular night, I was walking around my neighborhood, clearing my head from the day. There's something about getting out into fresh air that helps clear the mind. As I was walking down the paseo, I happened to look up at the moon. This night happened to have a full moon. It was truly breathtaking. The moon, being completely full this night, sparked a thought. *Wow! The moon is literally a perfect circle.* This thought provoked another thought. *OMG. All the planets are perfect circles.* Now, watch this domino effect of thoughts. *God made all of the planets perfectly. God doesn't ever mess up on the things He creates. God created me.* And finally, *God didn't mess up creating me.* Now, it's important to note that throughout my life, I really struggled with self-worth. It took me a really long time to get a sense of how valuable I am. This thought of God creating me and not messing up when He created me wrecked me in that moment. I believe that this chain reaction of thoughts was inspired by God's spirit and was indeed Him speaking to me. You can think what you'd like, but why not entertain the thought of there being an all-powerful, all-knowing, all-loving God that desires to speak to you? God's voice is beautiful. When you receive Jesus as your Lord and Savior, not only is relationship with your Creator restored and you get to spend eternity with Him. You have an opportunity to have a personal relationship or partnership with His Holy Spirit here and now. It is through the Holy Spirit that God speaks to us.

Don't worry, friend. I haven't forgotten about Samuel. You might be asking yourself, "Why did he open up this chapter talking about Samuel and then start on this tangent about God's voice?" Well, welcome to my brain. If you've ever had a conversation with me or heard me preach, the style of my writing won't surprise you at all. There's never a dull moment inside my noggin. That's a FACT. So back to Samuel. One of the first stories we read about Samuel as he is growing up in the temple is a really comical interaction between Samuel and God. Samuel was knocked out one night when it's as if God prank-called Samuel. God calls out to Samuel, and Samuel wakes up thinking that his master, Eli, is calling him. Samuel bursts up and runs to Eli, only to realize that Eli never called him. Then God waits for Samuel to get back into bed, only to call him again. Convinced that Eli had called him again, he got up and ran to him. Yet again, Eli didn't say anything to Samuel. This exchange happened THREE TIMES before Eli realized that God was talking to Samuel. Prank calls from God. No matter how inconvenient the timing was, Samuel was always willing to get up and go when God called him. I believe it was that very obedience to God's call that opened up a clear line of communication between Samuel and God. It was this type of interaction between Samuel and God that defined Samuel's life. As Samuel grew old, there came a day that the people of Israel, God's people, demanded a king. Up to this point, they didn't have a single king because they relied on leaders and governors who relied solely on God. Of course, Samuel was kind of bummed out about this because he believed that God was supposed to be the king of His people, but God gave Samuel the green light to find and appoint a king. Through a series of God-ordained events, Samuel comes in contact with this dashing young guy that goes by the name of Saul. Saul was the one that God chose to be king over his people. Samuel and Saul had a, well, challenging relationship. There were many occasions where Samuel asked Saul to accomplish very specific God-directed tasks, and because of his insecurities and fear, Saul didn't follow through with them at all. There was one time in particular that was like the straw that broke the camel's back, for lack of a better illustrative terminology. God had given Saul orders to destroy this nation called Amalek. This nation opposed God's people in the past. His particular assignment was to destroy the entire Amalekite nation (literally, everything gone). Saul got an army together and waged war on the Amalekites, like he was directed to do. Except rather than destroying everything like God had commanded him to, he spared the king's life and kept everything that appealed to them. YOU HAD ONE JOB, SAUL. The Bible even said that Saul and his army only destroyed the things that were worthless to them or of poor quality. Thanks, Saul. The next day, Samuel went to meet with Saul. When Samuel finally found Saul, it was obvious that he didn't do what God had commanded him to do. It reminds me of this one time that

Karen and I came home from running errands to find that our dog, Dallas, had gotten into the trash and ate an entire old loaf of bread from Cheesecake Factory. He greeted us so joyfully when we came in through the door and then tried to play it off all cool when I realized there was trash on the ground. I heard him saying through his demeanor "It was NOT me, Dad." I might have believed him, except there was a bunch of crumbs all over his face. It was OBVIOUS that Dallas had done something he wasn't supposed to. It was obvious that he ate an entire loaf of bread. As obvious as it was for me to know that Dallas ate the bread, that's how obvious it was for Samuel to realize that Saul had disobeyed God. Saul was supposed to destroy everything, remember? Yeah, except for the fact that there were livestock that he kept around right behind him when Samuel found him. The best part? Saul DENIED IT! He even talked up how well he and his army did at destroying everything. I mean, come on, bro. If you messed up, just own it! The more you try to hide it, the worse it's going to be for you. Samuel and Saul went back and forth, back and forth, and then finally Saul broke down and started to beg for forgiveness. This is, for real, like a scene out of an epic war movie. Samuel demands that Saul brings out the king of Amalek, the one he spared from the battle. Remember? This is the one that was originally supposed to be killed by Saul. Saul brings out the king, and Samuel kills him himself! What a boss! Reading through this story, it is so evident that this situation weighed heavily on Samuel's heart. It totally makes sense when you really think about it. This young man, who God used to pour into and anoint to be king over God's people, continues to fail because of his pride. Not only is he letting the people down and not doing what God tells him to do. He is LYING ABOUT IT! Of course, that would weigh heavy on anyone's heart.

The Bible says that after this exchange, Samuel never went to meet with Saul again, but he mourned constantly for him. I'm positive that Samuel was upset, hurt, disappointed, and just downright sad. This is someone that he had poured his life into. This is something that he put his complete trust and confidence in, only to be let down. Have you ever been there? A time in your life when you felt completely let down? I know I have. Maybe someone that you love hurt you. Maybe someone that you trusted completely to keep you safe betrayed that trust. Maybe someone in your family, who you love immensely, has been clean from drugs for years now but recently slipped up in a moment of weakness. Of course, you'd feel a sense of disappointment. When you're there in that space, it's hard to find the motivation to get up and move forward. It would be way easier to just sit and wallow in the pain. I know that's how Samuel felt. There's a scripture that pierced my heart in a way that I described earlier that was recorded right at this very moment of Samuel's life.

> Now the Lord said to Samuel, "You have mourned long enough for Saul. I have rejected him as king of Israel, so FILL YOUR FLASK with olive oil and go to Bethlehem. Find a man named Jesse who lives there, for I have selected one of his sons to be my King." (1 Samuel 16:1)

King David, just in case you haven't heard of him, is kind of a big deal. He's the one that God chose to be king after Saul. There is a time for mourning, absolutely. Mourning is such a healthy and necessary component to any healing process. But there comes a time in everyone who has experienced hurt or gone through heartbreak to make the bold decision to move forward, to fill their flask, to no longer let the bitterness define and consume them. David was patiently waiting for Samuel to get up, fill his flask, and move through the pain. Can I tell you that there are kings out there that are waiting for you to fill your flask? There are opportunities to be had. There is a beautiful life out there for you to live. As long as there is air in your lungs, there is a purpose for your life. There is more to life than Fortnite and Cheetos Puffs. You're never too far gone. This book is all about helping you move through challenges. Again, I'm not saying to not mourn. Please get help to mourn. You NEED to mourn. But there comes a time when you need someone to come alongside you, place their arm around you, and help you get up. God called me to write this book to help you get up and fill your flask to help you along in the healing process. Pain is a real thing. It's an inevitable part of life for anyone that isn't living under a rock. In this next chapter, I'll let you in on the experience that broke me. Or rather, the experience that forced me back together. I'll share with you the life-altering moments that sparked the fire in my heart to write this book for you. Brace yourself.

3

STAMPED

In life, there are moments that stamp you. I'm not talking about a literal stamp from the post office. You know what I'm talking about. Those unforgettable moments that stick with you. The first time you went on a plane. The first time that you sunk your teeth into thin-crust pizza in Little Italy, New York. The aftermath of that pizza on your lactose-intolerant stomach. Too much info? Don't act like you've never been there. Stamped. By the way, if the topic of poop makes you uncomfortable, you might want to put this book down now. I'm a youth pastor. Every other message I preach includes a poop illustration and how we are able to apply life-changing principles to our lives through it. Persistence Over Our Problems. Boom. POOP. You're welcome. Okay, Brandon. Back on track. Life-changing moments are moments that stamp you. The first time you rode a bike without training wheels. The first time you drove a car by yourself after getting your license. When you graduated high school or college. Everybody has their unique stamp stories. What's some stamp moments for you? For me, some moments that have stamped me was the first time I really met Jesus and the day I met Karen. Or should I say the day Karen and I were set up on a blind date? Stamped. That's a long story for later in the book, but I'll never forget that feeling I had in my heart the first moment I saw her in person. It feels like it was yesterday. Stamped. I'll also never forget the moment I knew I was going to propose to her. We were in line for Mr. Toad's Wild Ride at Disneyland when it hit me. Stamped. If you've ever been to Disneyland, you might be wondering, "Why that ride?" Well, Indiana Jones was super busy, and we were right next to the toad ride. I didn't feel like walking anymore. No big deal. Karen was visiting for a couple of weeks in December of 2017, and at this time, we had been dating for almost a year. In line, waiting for way too long for a three-minute ride, it hit me and hit me hard: it was time to propose. That moment of certainty, excitement, and anticipation. Stamped. Seeing her walk down the aisle with her mom and dad by her side at our wedding. Stamped. Stamping moments, in case you're wondering, can be both good and bad, of course. I'll never forget my first day of high school. My first class EVER was a math class. Now in high school, math classes usually have students from different grades in them. Unlike an English class that's designed specifically for freshmen, math classes have a nice little variety. First class, first day of my freshman year of high school, I sit down next to someone with a BEARD. A beard? Really? Coming from junior high, the only things that I was used to encountering were wispy moustaches and the smell of Axe body spray. Seeing someone with a straight-up beard legitimately freaked me out. Stamped. Sidenote: it took me until I was about thirty to grow a full beard. Even at thirty, there are high school students in my youth group that have better beards than I do. It is what it is. Stamped.

Now this next stamp is one that, in my opinion, has marked my life deeper than many other stamps. One night in October 2018, Karen was feeling a little uncomfortable. This feeling persisted for a couple of days, which led to us going to the store and buying our first ever pregnancy test. We had been trying to get pregnant for a little bit of time leading up to this, so we thought, could it be? I went alone to the store, and talk about an awkward moment. I'm not really sure why it was awkward. Maybe it was searching relentlessly in the same aisle of tampons as a guy. It could just be me. Anyways, I found the most expensive pregnancy test, which of course means most accurate, right? I found the kind that actually said pregnant, not those little lines. I didn't want any room for assumptions. I bought that bad boy and started my journey home. I took it in, gave it to Karen, and proceeded to wait. Moments later, we were stamped. That little expensive test said pregnant. My life was forever changed. Thoughts begin to race through my mind. *Is it a boy? Is it a girl? I kind of want a boy, but I kind of want a girl too. WHO AM I KIDDING? I'M A FREAKING DAD.* Fun fact: we actually knew we were pregnant before we knew we were pregnant. One of Karen's friends from Guatemala had a dream about Karen being pregnant on the actual day of conception and told us about it the morning following the dream. It wasn't until a couple of weeks after this that we actually found out we were pregnant for real. Talk about a TRIP. Okay, Jesus. I see you. Finding out that Karen and I were pregnant was beyond exciting. It was mind-bending actually. It didn't really hit me until the day that we heard our little baby's heart for the first time.

All the talk in our world today about when life begins, in all honesty, breaks my heart. I won't spend time in this book arguing a point, but I must say that hearing a live rhythmic beat coming from inside your wife's belly after only six weeks of development opens your eyes WIDE.

I didn't know if the baby was a boy or girl. It honestly didn't matter to me. I didn't know if they were going to play music like dad, be really artistic like mom, or athletic like, well, not really anyone in my family. It didn't matter. They could be whoever they wanted to be. More specifically, I was excited to be a witness of them discovering who God designed them to be. Excited was actually a severe understatement.

Time passed by, faster than ever. Four weeks turned into eight, and eight turned into sixteen in the blink of an eye. We became familiar with the doctor's office. Our nurse knew us, and we knew her. We were even on a first-name basis with her, no big deal. Do nurses go by their last name? Do they even tell us their names? Not important because I felt SPECIAL. At our six-week appointment, they introduced us to the most awkward device in the history of the practice of medicine, the ultrasound. All I have to say is poor Karen. Even though this was SO uncomfortable for everyone involved, something life-changing happened. We got to see our baby. No facial features, obviously, but we saw our baby. I was stamped. Stamped and in love.

This tiny, little dot on the screen was mine and Karen's baby. Crazy to think that in about eight months from that moment, I'd be holding him or her in my arms. That little bean would have a face, personality, arms, legs, and hair. They would be perfect, and I couldn't wait. The same appointment that we got to see our little bean baby for the very first time was also the appointment that we got to hear their heart. Like I said a bit ago, I feel like this whole experience didn't hit me until I heard their tiny heartbeat. It was faint, quick, and perfectly in time. Did I mention that it was perfectly in time? In that moment, I was CONVINCED that my little baby would be a musician or a dancer or a singer. I decided that for them. Hearing their heartbeat caused mine to skip a beat. It went from being an exciting idea to a life-changing, mind-spinning reality. I was in love. I was stamped.

The nurse printed out a little paper with our baby's picture on it along with the rhythm of their heart. Needless to say, I was ready to tell the world. I was ready to frame that bad boy up and put it all over our house. I was ready to blog about this experience, preach about this experience, SCREAM about this experience, but I now know there's a process that needs to take place before that can happen. I swear I was ready to post a picture on my Instagram the moment I stepped foot out of the doctor's office, but again, there are necessary steps involved in sharing this kind of news with the world. Karen schooled me in this.

I took that glossy paper printout, held it in disbelief and awe, and pressed it to my heart. "This will be the most exciting and life-changing experience ever, and we are ready," I said to Karen. We smiled at each other, held each other's hands, and began to pray. Our prayer was simple and yet so profound.

"Jesus, this baby is a gift from You, and we dedicate them back. Use their life to bring You glory and honor. Thank You for trusting us."

We were ready to be parents.

If you've ever been through a pregnancy or known someone who has, you are familiar with how they do the checkups. Some are intrusive, others not so much. Exciting, scary, unfamiliar, so much medical terminology infiltrating my brain it felt like it was on the verge of exploding constantly. Similar feelings to how I felt in algebra. With each new week, we learned more and more about our baby. Karen had downloaded this LEGIT app on her phone that told us how big the baby was and what part of their body was specifically developing that week. Can we pause briefly and acknowledge the fact that there is literally an app for EVERYTHING? Calculator? App for that. Need to order some food? App for that. How did we ever survive without smartphones? Anyways, Karen downloaded this app, which kept us up-to-date with how big our baby was getting and what was uniquely developing that week. I must say, the weeks that compared my baby to fruit and vegetables made me feel SO awkward every time I ate the fruit or vegetable that coincided with my baby's size for that week. I'll never look at salads the same. I know I wasn't eating a baby, but it kind of felt like it. Not only did the app tell you how big your baby was. It told you what part of your baby was developing, which, for people who pray, adds an extremely unique and special dynamic to covering your baby in prayer. For example, there was a week that we learned that our baby's brain was developing. Our prayer went along the lines of, "Lord, this week You are developing our baby's brain. We pray that you strengthen their mind. May they always know Your voice and be familiar with You. We pray that as their brain is wired together, piece by piece, layer by layer, it would be fixed on You always. Make them smart. Make them funny. Their mind is dedicated to You. Amen." Pretty cool, right? I really encourage you, if ever you get the opportunity to do this, do it. To be involved in every aspect of your baby's life and development, even before they take their first breath, is an extremely special experience.

This was a fun season. Karen and I started to literally switch up and adapt every area of our lives. Bigger car, check. Bigger apartment, check. Every trip to Target involved a thirty-minute detour to the baby section to start researching cribs, car seats, bottles, diapers, you name it. We searched it all thoroughly. Usually when we go to Target, I try to get in and out as quickly as possible (as is all guys' mission). But in all honesty, I didn't mind looking at baby merchandise at all. I wanted the best for this baby. This baby is about to be straight-up SPOILED. Unashamedly so. Judge me.

Time passed on by, and days turned into weeks. Weeks quickly turned to months. Karen and I were about to conclude our first trimester of pregnancy, and I couldn't believe it. I'm pretty sure that time accelerates starting the moment of conception. Science doesn't prove this yet, but I am convinced of it. It felt like there was now forty seconds in a minute rather than sixty. This is the same phenomenon that takes place when you need to get something done and you're running out of time. Or on days off. Think about it. At this point in the process, Karen and I hadn't told many people about our baby. We wanted to wait until after the first trimester to tell anyone really because we've read the statistics about how much the risk goes down after the first trimester. You never want to think about that kind of stuff, but it's a reality in the world we live in, and we didn't want to put it out there and need to explain anything to anyone if something terrible were to happen. You understand.

As we concluded our first trimester, we were nearing Christmastime, which obviously meant, being married to Karen, that we were going to do something SO cute to announce it to our families. Socks? No. Picture? No. Song? Definitely not. Hello, guys. It's CHRISTMAS. Let's get our family a precious ornament that says "Baby Maurizio coming 2019!" And, friends, let me tell you. A precious ornament is what we got. It was so stinking cute it made puppies look ugly. We got one for my Dad and stepmom, one for my mom, and one for Karen's parents back in Guatemala. At this time, Karen's brother was in town spending Christmas with us, so we wanted to tell him before we started giving the ornaments out. We also wanted him in on everything so that he can film the moment when he gave it to Karen's parents when he went back home. Let me tell you how we told him too because it was stinkin' cute. I went to Starbucks, like always, and got myself, Karen, and Karen's brother, Carlos, a grande hot peppermint mocha. By the way, that's the BEST drink during the holiday season at Starbucks. I realize that they have both peppermint and mocha all year round, but it's just not the same. I picked up the drinks and made my way back to our little place. Before I went back inside, I busted out a sharpie in the car and wrote on his cup "Uncle Carlos." Under his name I put, "You're the first one in the family to find out WE ARE PREGNANT." The look on his face when he began to understand what was happening was absolutely priceless. Watching him read it was such a special moment. I think I even cried. That says a lot. I rarely cried. There really was so much joy, excitement, and anticipation that filled our hearts as we began to dream together as a family about that coming day in September of 2019 when we would welcome our little baby into this world. From that moment on, Karen and I enlisted Carlos as our private spy and assistant. He aided us in dropping that bomb of news on everyone in our family that we planned for. On Christmas morning of 2018, we gifted both my mom and my dad with the announcement ornament. We filmed their reactions, but if only I could see another recording of this moment from the perspective of what my face looked like. It was probably like the goofiest smile, with eyes that were locked on to someone, waiting for them to discover something you left for them. Those moments were beautiful. The joy on my dad's face when he realized what it was we were announcing was so pure. It was his first grandchild. Of COURSE, it's time to celebrate. His smile was so big, ear to ear, and of course, that was contagious. We laughed, cried, celebrated, and ultimately gave thanks to God. This was, no doubt, a gift from Him. After we celebrated on Christmas morning with my dad and stepmom, it was time to bring the news to my mom. As to be expected, there was nothing but surprise, excitement, and anticipation. With the amount of celebration and happiness that was going down, I wouldn't be surprised if neighbors on both sides of her house were aware of what was happening. The joy was so tangible it most likely seeped through the walls. A week or so passed after that, and it was time for Carlos to go home back to Guatemala. As soon as Carlos landed and got home, he gave our ornament gift to Karen's parents and filmed it. It was so sweet to see their reactions. It was their first grandchild as well. Now usually, when any of us make the trip from US to Guatemala, a nap is necessary before anything else can take place. Carlos really gave us a solid by pulling this through. Flying without naps is HARD. Believe me, I've tried to go to dinners or meetings right after we land in Guatemala, and let me just say I'm not entirely there. My body is present, but my mind is far from it. I really do wish that I could sleep on planes. There's something about being thousands of feet in the air, going extremely fast in a metal tube, and being flown by someone I've never met that creates an unsettling sense in my soul. No matter how many consecutive movies I watch, how many fluffy little pillows they give me, or how many sleepy pills I take prior to boarding, I can't sleep. To add to the situation, nine out of ten flights to Guatemala I've ever taken are red-eye flights. Let me tell you, the name holds true.

The deed was done. All our immediate family was in the know as to what was going on in mine and Karen's life. Even after all the announcements, it still felt like a dream to me. Stamped. As time continued to move forward, the plans of revealing the news to our kids at the church was our next big milestone. Once the students knew, there was no turning back. Rather than taking six months to tell them all individually and risk some of them not hearing first and getting all mad, we did what any pregnant youth pastor would do and made an announcement to the kids on a Sunday morning. It got real. We needed to wait until the end of service to make the announcement, of course. It's already challenging enough without baby announcements to retain the students' attention on a Sunday morning when ninety percent of them wish they were still at home asleep in bed. Imagine how hard it would be to refocus the message if we made the announcement at the beginning of service. It would be harder to do that than it would be to capture and train a wild goose. Have you ever tried to interact with a goose in the wild? If you know, you know. They are FIESTY. We set it up and then dropped the news on the kids, all nonchalant. I'm pretty sure some of them were still asleep when we gave the announcement. That's how smooth it was. The kids who caught it were shocked! Even the ones that usually never said a word to us on a Sunday morning came up to us after and congratulated us. With each passing day, with every moment that flew by, it was becoming more and more real. I couldn't wait for all these people to meet this beautiful baby in person. We were six months away and counting.

As we progressed through the weeks, we had to go see our baby nurse once every four weeks. On the eighth week and twelfth week, it was routine checkups. We went in, and Karen was intruded by that awkward machine. We either saw our little bean baby (it looked like a little bean on the ultrasound screen), or we had the opportunity hear their heartbeat. That was honestly a sound I never got tired of hearing. Every beat was perfect, and with every thump, that little baby propelled deeper and deeper into my heart. I was so in love. Karen and I couldn't wait until our week twenty appointment because that was the week when we were going to learn our baby's gender. Like I mentioned earlier, I didn't mind whether it was a boy or a girl; I was just beyond joyed to be a father. I know some people say they would rather have a boy over a girl or the other way around. Again, I was blessed to have either. Preparation for this little nugget to arrive was already well underway. Karen and I had the opportunity to get a bigger car, and we just pulled the trigger on moving into a bigger apartment. Our little pool house, which was our first place, was quaint and all, but the thought of having a newborn there with us and the dog didn't seem too ideal. We searched around and found a perfect one-bedroom, one-loft apartment right down the street from where we worked. Everything was happening SO fast. It's like the momentum had begun, and there was no stopping it. From the moment we made the announcement to our parents, it was like time accelerated. Fast forward (see what I did there?) to February 16. This was a Saturday in 2019, and it just so happened to be Karen's birthday. Not only was it her birthday; it was the day when we moved into our new apartment. The entire week prior to this day was rain like California hadn't seen in a very long time. We weren't looking forward to moving in the rain, but you gotta do what you gotta do, you know? The Friday night prior to our move was looking ominous, and the grey clouds were filling every inch of the sky. With every breath in, it was like you could taste the rain brewing in the air. When we woke up on Saturday morning to go pick up the U-Haul, very much to our surprise, there wasn't a cloud in the sky. It was as if God parted the rain clouds for us to move without any hindrances. Have you read the story in the Bible when God literally makes the sun stand still? Yeah, it kind of felt like that same sort of thing went down. No joke. We did the move and settled in, and then it started raining almost immediately after that. Some would call that a coincidence. I choose to look at it as God making His provision for us exceedingly obvious. As the dust settled on the day of our move and all our helping hands had gone home, Karen and I sat on the carpet, boxes surrounding us, and realized that our dream of becoming parents was becoming more of a reality in each and every moment. There was an upstairs loft in our new apartment that was going to be a perfect sanctuary for our little baby to spend its first months of life in. This was getting real. Stamped.

The Monday after we moved in to our apartment, we had our sixteen-week checkup. These are, historically, really easy, smooth appointments. We make our appointments on Mondays because working in ministry, Mondays are practically the only day off you get. Mondays are perfect days for baby checkups to happen. We pulled in to our normal spot in the parking structure, walked the short little walk to our doctor's suite, signed in, and waited to get called into our room. Business as usual. Our nurse, Kitty (we were on a first-name basis, remember?), called us into our room to get us ready to have our checkup. She was a very sweet lady, very caring, and beyond nurturing. She was the perfect kind of nurse. You know how sometimes you get nurses that give off the "I'd rather be anywhere else but here" vibe? Kitty made you feel like you were the only patient she had of the day. Never rushed and always gave you her full attention. She sat us down like every other appointment, busted out that extremely awkward machine, the ultrasound, and started to press it firmly against Karen's belly. A couple moments passed by, and we didn't hear anything. Not something to be alarmed of though. She assured us that sometimes it takes a couple tries to get the right angle. She kept searching, and nothing was happening. When we should have heard the beautiful heartbeat of our baby, we then heard a deafening silence. Though Kitty was a very mild-mannered individual, it was obvious that there was a sense of concern beginning to manifest. The tension in the room became so thick you could cut it with a knife. She looked at us and said, "This kind of thing happens all of the time! Especially after lunch." She handed Karen a cup of water and instructed her to walk around the hallways for a bit.

By doing this, it would reposition the baby and make the heartbeat prominent in the ultrasound reading. Kitty stepped out of the room for a moment. I looked over at my wife and saw that fear started to take hold of her. I stood up, went over to her, held her, and started to pray. "God, you have a plan for this baby. You spoke to us and gave us so many confirmations for this baby. We even prayed every single night for this baby's development. Thank you that you're with us, God. We need a miracle right now." No sooner than I finished praying the prayer, Kitty walked back into our room. This time, she brought a way more intrusive machine. Karen sat down, and Kitty started to again search for a heartbeat. Karen didn't speak a word the whole time. She didn't have to. I, full of faith, was expecting to hear my baby's heartbeat, but instead, I heard silence. Every second felt like an hour, and it was creeping by ever so slowly. Kitty looked at us, said nothing definitive, and invited us to go downstairs to a different testing room to get some definitive answers. As soon as she powered down her machine, my stomach sank to the floor. Though she told us nothing, Karen and I began to brace ourselves for the worst possible news. We went downstairs to the testing room, where they put us through yet another ultrasound. Only this time around, there were no smiles. There were no sounds of celebration. The nurse's demeanor that was helping us was very somber. Instead of the classic fluorescent doctor office lighting, we were in a room that had warm lighting. It was as if they were trying to calm us down and sooth our emotions before receiving the worst news imaginable. But yet again, they said nothing. They set us up with another appointment in a couple of hours to go back to our original nurse, Kitty. Karen and I left the doctor's office and walked the longest walk to our car. As soon as we got into the car, Karen broke down crying. I didn't cry. I'm pretty sure I was in denial of what was happening. "They didn't tell us anything definitive yet." I kept trying to comfort myself and Karen. We tried to go get smoothies to pass the time, but let's be honest, an appetite was the farthest thing from us.

A couple of hours passed, and we made our way back to Kitty. Usually, Kitty would greet us with a giant smile. This time, she was very serious. We sat down in our room, and she began to explain to us that our baby's little heart wasn't beating. No matter what angle they tried to hear it at, it wasn't making a sound. She explained that they tried multiple machines to find a result. Even the faintest heartbeat would have sufficed, but again, nothing. The testing room we went to downstairs actually wasn't a testing room. It was the place where they measured our baby to see how old it was when it stopped growing. Our little baby was supposed to be the size of a sixteen-week-old. Instead, it was the size of about fourteen weeks. Our baby was already in heaven for two weeks by the time we received this news. It hit us like a ton of bricks. No. It actually felt like someone ripped my heart out of my chest, threw it on the ground, and started to stomp on it. I didn't know what to feel. I didn't know what to think. I didn't know what to believe. All I knew at the time is that I had to be there for Karen. Our nurses said their condolences and got us an appointment that same afternoon to go to the hospital and undergo a procedure to get the baby's body out of Karen. This can't be real life.

It was Monday, February 18, that we received the news that our precious little baby was no longer with us here on earth. In the time between our nurse appointment and our newly scheduled doctor's appointment, we went over to my dad's house to simply be with someone. Not to receive counsel or advice but to just be. He and my stepmom happened to be home from work that day because it was Presidents' Day. As soon as my stepmom opened the door, her usual happy-to-see-her-kids smile quickly faded to concern when she realized something was wrong with us. Karen, with tears in her eyes, said four words that I thought I'd never hear: "We lost the baby." Karen collapsed into her arms, and my dad came rushing in from the back room as soon as he realized something was wrong. Nothing about this entire experience felt like reality. We waited there for two and a half hours before getting a call back from the doctor's office informing us that we were able to come by and check ourselves in. Every moment felt as though a piece of my heart was chipping away. I didn't know what to feel. All I knew at the time is that I needed to be there for Karen. We went to the hospital and checked in to the maternity wing. Walking down the long, coldly lit hallway, looking at the pictures of babies on the walls, we finally made it to our room. It was dark and lonely, or maybe that's just what my perceived memory of it was. Karen got into her bed, and we then met the nurse that was going to be with us for the duration of this experience. It was five in the afternoon. After about an hour's worth of filling out forms and signing waivers, we finally got to meet our doctor. He was a nice man, but I feel as though he didn't really know what to say or how to interact with us. Honestly, that's totally okay. As long as you're a good doctor, you don't even need to say a word to us. He introduced himself and gave us a lowdown on what to anticipate in this experience. Now, since having gone through this, it truly is mind-blowing to me to hear stories from so many people that have gone through something similar. Though I haven't heard the same story, the pain in losing a baby is still so real for anyone that goes through that. If you're reading this, having gone through a miscarriage or abortion, I want you to know that you're not alone. Please reach out to someone and walk with them through this! I'll never forget the next words that the doctor said to us. "We will give you some medicine that will cause your body to go into labor and deliver the baby. If it doesn't work in the next six hours, we will give you another dose of it." That's when it hit me. We weren't going to go home tonight. I called my mom and let her know what was going on, and like the superhero that she is, she jumped right into action and took care of our dog for the next couple of days. After receiving the medicine, Karen's body slowly started to go into labor. The pain got worse and worse, until right at 12:32 a.m. the next morning, Karen gave birth to our baby boy. When the nurse finished helping us through that moment, Karen and I learned that she had just given birth to a boy. Remember, Karen and I weren't going to learn the gender of our baby for another four weeks. That piece of knowledge came a tad earlier than we'd both have liked it to. We had a name picked out for a girl and a name picked out for a boy. In that moment, as the nurse held the little body of our baby boy in the dark, cold hours on the morning of February 19, 2019, we met our son, Asher Maurizio, for the first time. I saw his hands, his fingers, his arms, his legs, his little feet and toes, his face, his nose, his head. He was beginning to form into a little person. It was more than just a cluster of tissue. This was our son. Words will never begin to encompass the emotion that surfaced from this long, dreadful night. Questions that will never have answers. Hurt, anger, doubt, fear are all circling violently around my thoughts. We didn't leave the hospital until three in the afternoon, nearing twenty-seven hours from when the whole experience began to unfold. It came without warning, hurt beyond compare, and flipped our world upside down. Isn't that true of any type of traumatic event? You can't see it coming. It hits you hard and leaves you picking up pieces of your broken heart afterward. When we finally left the hospital, the nurse told me to go get the car and pick up Karen from the front driveway. This was hospital procedure. Up until that point, I never cried. I think I wanted to be strong and constant for Karen going through it or something like that. I finally arrived to our bigger car, the one we got for the baby, sat down in the driver's seat, took off my sunglasses, and started to weep. Images of the previous night bombarded my mind like a fire hose. I was broken. There are no other words to describe how I felt. Simply broken. I picked Karen up from the front of the hospital, and we drove back to our new apartment, the one that we also moved into because of the baby. We sat together in our parking space and just wept. We were supposed to have that trip with a baby. We were supposed to come home from the hospital with a baby. Having spoken with a lot of women who had gone through labor, they've told me that the single thing that makes it worth it is the moment when you get to hold your baby at the end of the pain. That wasn't the case for us. There was no closure and no reward for the pain. This was ground zero. This was the aftermath of a bomb that was hurled into mine and Karen's lives. Though this was, by far, the most brutal experience we've ever walked through, somehow, we knew that God was with us. I'll never forget sitting in the hospital room in my super uncomfortable chair when the lyrics of the song "Goodness of God" by Bethel started to play in my mind. "All my life You have been faithful. All my life You have been so, so good. With every breath that I am able, I will sing of the goodness of God. Your goodness is running after. It's running after me. With my life laid down, I surrender now. I give you everything. Your goodness is running after, it keeps running after me." I knew that no matter how dark this situation looked like, no matter how alone I felt, God was with us. The Bible talks about how the peace that comes from God doesn't make any sense. This couldn't be truer than it was in the current circumstances. It hurt, believe me. It hurt like hell. But even in the hurt, God's peace secured our hearts. This was the beginning of my through journey.

Death never comes at a convenient time. I've spoken at the funeral of a gentleman in his nineties, who was married to his wife for seventy years. I've attended the funeral of a teenage boy that took his own life, and I now know what it's like to lose your baby before the day they take their first breath. The common thread that holds these experiences together is the feeling of never having enough time. Regardless of what you believe about eternity and life after death, the reality of not having this person with you in this life anymore really hurts. It always does. Of course, I believe with my whole heart that Karen and I are going to see and hold Asher in heaven someday, but that doesn't make our loss here on earth any less devastating. Quick piece of encouragement for anyone reading this that never knows what to do for someone that just experienced loss: don't give advice. Don't even worry about saying anything for that matter. Don't try to come up with an explanation as to why it happened. Just be with them. Mine and Karen's dogs are such a serious source of support, and they have never given us advice. They are simply with us. Death never comes at a convenient time.

Heartache is part of life. Loss is part of life. I believe it's something that everyone on this earth has in common. Though it looks different in every story, it's something that can bind our hearts together. For one person, it's the loss of a loved one. For another, it can be your parents or a friend going through divorce. It can be the loss of a job, the dissolving of a relationship, sexual abuse growing up, and so many more scenarios. As you read this, you might be thinking of your unique experiences with loss and heartache. Your brain also might be trying so hard to bury those emotions as quickly as they come up. I know that's what mine does whenever I try to think about my parents getting divorced. I can only recall a few specific moments from the entire process. Crazy, right? Now, we've established that we all have the common ground of hurt. What we don't all have in common though is how we process through the pain. Some individuals are great at addressing and confronting hurts when they happen, but the 99.080 percent of the rest of us have to learn how to go through them in a way that isn't completely detrimental to our health. Trust me, with losing Asher, I tried my best to run from the pain, to not feel it, to press on in life as though nothing ever happened. This, of course, didn't work. As much as I tried going around it, it was only a matter of time until I was forced to go through it. Anxiety, panic attacks, and depression slowly chipped away at the pride that kept me from acknowledging my need for help. When I couldn't take the pain anymore and I was too tired to keep pretending like I was okay, I finally accepted the inevitability of going through it. The longer you wait to go through the dark times in life, the deeper the pain will be. The choice is yours as to when you will decide to go through it. Take it from someone that's well-acquainted with pain and even more acquainted with trying to run from it. It's better to face it and begin moving forward one step at a time than it is to run from and ignore it. I know you might not want to, but it's better to do what you know is right and feel good later than it is to wait to feel good to do what you know is right. This book is designed for you. It was written with you in mind. I'll share with you what I learned along the journey. We are going to go through this together.

The next portion of this book will be broken into three sections that are derived from a passage of Scripture found in Isaiah 43:2. It says, "When you go through deep waters, I will be with you. When you go through rivers of difficulty, you will not drown. When you walk through the fire of oppression, you will not be burned up; the flames will not consume you."

This scripture was and continues to be an anchor for my soul. It came to me at just the right time. Notice how it says the word *when* and not the word *if*. It would be nice if it said "if" because then it leaves the option open to not go through things. The reality of this scripture is that it says "when." It's not a matter of if we go through challenging times. It's a matter of when we go through challenging times. We can not only count on that, but we can count on what the scripture promises in the latter. He will be with us, and it will not be the end of our story. Together, we will take a look at going through the storm, the fire, and the valley. Each element closely relates to things we walk through in life. My prayer for you is that as you read the words in this book, in each of the sections, it will not only set you free, but it will begin to start the process of healing. Let's get ready to go through.

STORM

When you go THROUGH DEEP WATERS, I will be with you. When you go through rivers of difficulty, you will not drown. When you walk through the fire of oppression, you will not be burned up; the flames will not consume you. (Isaiah 43:2, emphasis added)

4

THE STORM IS NECESSARY

We don't do storms in sunny California. Sure, we get fires and earthquakes more than some other locations around the country, but we don't do storms. The light drizzle that we experience in California is a laughing matter when compared to the storms that others around the world experience. We Californians literally have no idea what to do when it starts to rain more than a sprinkle. People lose their minds while driving, begin stocking up on nonperishable foods, and start looking for a guy building an ark, and anyone you come into interaction with seems to be on edge. "Please don't cuss at me, ma'am. I didn't mean to take the last can of corn. Oh, that's right. It's raining." In all honesty, I actually like the rain. There's something about putting on a silky robe, striking up a fire in the fireplace, brewing up a fresh cup of coffee, and busting out a good Netflix session while it's raining outside. It does the soul good. Let me clarify, I like when it's raining outside and I don't need to go anywhere. For some reason, if ever I get wet in the rain and it's under sixty degrees outside, nine times out of ten, I'll get sick. Don't judge me. I grew up in California. When Karen and I first got married, there was a time when a storm was forecasted to roll through the place we lived. In the morning on this particular day, there was light rain, but after we had arrived at the church offices, it began to really come down. Like, really come down. This type of rain was, for sure, beyond a typical California rain. Karen wasn't fazed by this whatsoever. Keep in mind,

Karen is from Guatemala. Guatemala has real rain, and life doesn't stop if the storms get intense there. I have memories of talking to Karen on FaceTime when we were dating, and she was driving a stick, putting on makeup, eating her breakfast, and doing her hair, all while it's pouring down rain! California rain is nothing compared to Guatemala rain. The rain gradually got more and more intense here on that day. Thunder started booming in the distance, even so much so to where we felt a slight rumble in our office building. When the rainfall hit a climax, I was so intrigued by how hard it was coming down that I was compelled to get out of my chair and make my way to the upstairs common area. In that space, there is a large window that spans from the top of the ceiling all the way to the floor. I knew that it would be a prime location to view this epic rainfall. Then again, this isn't something you see in sunny California that often. I was mesmerized. I looked down from the window and saw sheet after sheet of water falling from the sky. It was falling so hard and so heavy that I was convinced I was going to see some people cruise on by in a canoe. I was so encapsulated by this rare phenomenon. I didn't even realize that everyone else that had their office on the second floor came out and joined me in staring out the window. We were all immersed in the experience. It was as if we were all seeing something for the very first time. We were hypnotized, all of us. Then my moment of serenity was brought to an abrupt conclusion by the sound of laughter. My sweet moment was shot down by my sweet wife, who, while violently giggling, proceeded to film us all for her Instagram story. She was getting a kick out of the Californians obsessing over rain. "I'm so glad this brought so much joy to your heart, love." I get it. Us Californians don't know what real storms look like. Let's be honest, the only people in California that are well prepared for rain are the ones that move to California from somewhere else. You can spot the ones who were born here a mile away! Next time it's raining and you happen to find yourself in a place with other people, look out for the ones either wearing shorts or running rapidly from their car due to leaving their umbrella at home. I openly admit to fitting in those categories on a majority of the times it rains, with me only having an umbrella when it rains roughly one out of ten times. Good thing it only rains about ten times a year in California.

The Sunday after we moved in to our new apartment, literally the second day we were entirely in there, it began to rain again. Remember how I told you that on the week of our move-in day, it rained nonstop, excluding the actual day of our move? Yeah, it's as if Mother Nature stored up rain on that Saturday and unloaded a nice healthy dose of it on Sunday. We went to church, like we always did on Sundays, and when we got back to our new (I'll say it again, NEW apartment), I heard a sound coming from the far right corner of our living room. An ever so angelic pitter-patter. I look over to my right, and there it was—a nice, soggy puddle that was beginning to form on our carpet. I then looked up at the ceiling, only to discover a patched spot that has clearly had some previous work done to it. REALLY? Just what we needed, something to address in an apartment that we just moved in to. Was this a foreshadowing of things to come? The rain, even though it gave birth to an extremely irritating situation, revealed to us that there was a part of our apartment that needed to be fixed. There was a piece of our ceiling that wasn't operating the way it should. That crack in our ceiling was always there. We just weren't aware of it until it started raining. In our lives, there is brokenness, brokenness that we might not ever know about until it starts to rain.

The scripture in Isaiah 43:2 says that though we go through deep waters, God will be with us. This chapter will reveal what real life storms can symbolically look like, how we can navigate through them, and ultimately, how to change our perspective of the storm. If we can begin to change our perspective of the storms we go through, those storms actually have the potential to strengthen us rather than tear us down. Maybe right now you feel as though you're living your life underwater. You can't seem to catch a breath. Every time you catch a day or two to rest, it's like circumstances jump on you twice as hard and forces your head down again. The wind and the waves are daunting, and you can't find any peace. I have good news for you, my friend. You're not alone in this.

Perspective is everything. In fact, perspective has the power to determine whether or not you will become bitter or better when storms come. There's a guy in the Bible that was highly acquainted with storms, both literal and metaphorical. His name is Paul, the apostle. This guy is a true champion. Not only did he go all over the place starting churches and spreading the good news about Jesus. He wrote about three-fourths of what we now know as the New Testament. Many of the books in the New Testament are letters that Paul wrote to the churches he started. For example, the book of Philippians is a letter that Paul wrote to the church in Philippi. The book of Ephesians was a letter that Paul wrote to the church in Ephesus. Corinthians, Corinth and Romans, Rome. You get the picture. If you read through the book of Acts, you'll get a glimpse into the life and ministry of Paul. It's CRAZY. Here's his ministry in a nutshell. Paul used to go by the name Saul. Saul was a member of an elite group of religious teachers called the Pharisees. If you ever heard a story about Jesus getting into an argument with someone, it probably was involving a Pharisee. The Pharisees would persecute the early Christian church, even to the point of death in some cases. Saul was so passionate about persecuting anyone that was following the message of Jesus. The Bible even says in Acts 8:3 that he went from house to house, dragging out both men and women to throw them into prison. It says in Acts 9:1 that he uttered threats with every breath that he took and was eager to kill the Lord's followers. This was a bad dude. He was viciously dedicated to seeing the church dismantled and destroyed. On a day just like any other day, Saul was on his way to a city called Damascus to bombard all the synagogues there and rid them of Christians. While he was on his way there, he had a life-altering encounter. On this particular day, he met Jesus. Literally met Jesus. Keep in mind, this happened after Jesus died, resurrected, and ascended to heaven. While Saul was cruising on down the road, a light from heaven beamed down all around him and knocked him off his donkey. Jesus called him out and commissioned him in that very moment. Jesus was imploring him to use the same passion he had toward destroying the church to now build the church. Not only did God change his name to Paul that day. Everything about who he was changed as well. I truly do believe one encounter with God can change the course of someone's life in an instant. Also, if at this moment you feel as though you've done too many bad things for God to love you and use you to change the world, just look at the story of Paul. God took someone who was a murderer, a CHRISTIAN killer, and used him in a magnificent way. There's literally nothing you can do to disqualify yourself from God's plan for you. Paul is a beautiful example and reminder of this truth. As you read through the New Testament, it's truly mind-blowing to learn how many hardships Paul went through. Not only did he go through them. It's as if he grew personally stronger and closer to God each time. If you want to feel better about your life, just take some time to look at Paul's. He says the following to the church of Corinth:

> I have worked harder, been put in prison more often, been whipped times without number, and faced death again and again. Five different times the Jewish leaders gave me thirty-nine lashes. Three times I was beaten with rods. Once I was stoned. Three times I was shipwrecked. Once I spent a whole night and a day adrift at sea. I have traveled on many long journeys. I have faced danger from rivers and from robbers. I have faced danger from my own people, the Jews, as well as from the Gentiles. I have faced danger in the cities, in the deserts, and on the seas. And I have faced danger from men who claim to be believers but are not. I have worked hard and long, enduring many sleepless nights. I have been hungry and thirsty and have often gone without food. I have shivered in the cold, without enough clothing to keep me warm. Then, besides all this, I have the daily burden of my concern for all the churches. Who is weak without my feeling that weakness? Who is led astray, and I do not burn with anger? (2 Corinthians 11:23–19)

Paul was no stranger to hard times. He goes on to say in the next chapter:

> I was given a thorn in my flesh, a messenger from Satan to torment me and keep me from becoming proud. Three different times I begged the Lord to take it away. Each time He said, "My grace is all you need. My power works best in weakness." So now I am glad to boast about my weaknesses, so that the power of Christ can work through me. That's why I take pleasure in my weakness, and in the insults, hardships, persecutions, and troubles that I suffer for Christ. For when I am weak, then I am strong. (2 Corinthians 12:7–10)

Paul mentions that he was whipped, beaten within inches of his life, flogged more times than he can count, came close to dying numerous times, was shipwrecked more than once, has had rocks hurled at him, has spent nights floating in the ocean, been exhausted from traveling, has faced danger in just about any environment and from just about any imaginable people group, has starved, almost froze to death, and has been imprisoned multiple times. Not only did he go through all of that physically. He carried mental burdens as well. I get exhausted just typing all of this out. I thought youth pastoring was challenging. Even through all this, Paul remained strong and faithful to God's calling over his life. How in the world was he able to do that? When Karen and I lost Asher, there were so many moments that I was so close to giving up. I fought the thoughts of *Is God truly with me? Is God truly for me?* How is it then that Paul goes through what seems like one thing after another and continues to move forward? Simply put, Paul had a healthy perspective.

Time and time again, throughout the letters that Paul wrote, we see themes of this perspective emerge. Here are a few examples:

> And I want you to know, my dear brothers and sisters, that everything that has happened to me

here has helped to spread the Good News. For everyone here, including the whole palace guard, knows that I am in chains because of Christ. And because of my imprisonment, most of the believers here have gained confidence and boldly speak God's message without fear. (Philippians 1:12–14)

Whatever happens, my dear brothers and sisters, rejoice in the Lord. I never get tired of telling you these things, and I do it to safeguard your faith. (Philippians 3:1)

Not that I was ever in need, for I have learned how to be content with whatever I have. I know how to live on almost nothing or with everything. I have learned the secret of living in every situation, whether it is with a full stomach or empty, with plenty or little. For I can do everything through Christ, who gives me strength." (Philippians 4:11–13)

We are pressed on every side by troubles, but we are not crushed. We are perplexed, but not driven to despair. We are hunted down, but never abandoned by God. We get knocked down, but we are not destroyed. Through suffering, our bodies continue to share in the death of Jesus so that the life of Jesus may also be seen in our bodies. (2 Corinthians 4:8–10)

With this filter applied to reading through the Bible, it's IMPOSSIBLE to miss it. Peter, one of the guys who walked with and followed Jesus closely during His earthy ministry, wrote a letter of encouragement to a group of Jesus followers who were experiencing extreme storms. When I say extreme, I mean extreme. At the time of this letter being written, the ruler that was in power was a guy by the name of Nero Claudius Caesar. Nero was a bad dude. It's honestly hard to wrap your mind around some of the things he had done to Christians. For example, he would take the skin off dead animals, drape them over the Christians, and release wild dogs to attack and eat them. If that's not bad enough, he would cover Christians in hot wax and hang them from trees as decorations for his parties. Keeping all this context in mind, Peter wrote the following to people faced with this type of hardship:

> So be truly glad. There is wonderful joy ahead,
> even though you must endure many trials for a
> little while. (1 Peter 1:6)

The Bible is full of people that went through challenging things throughout their lives here on earth. I'm confident in saying that every single person that is mentioned in the entire Bible narrative went through something hard at one point or another. There seems to be a clear and common theme. Hebrews 11 is a chapter that's known as the faith chapter. This chapter is filled with inspiring, encouraging, and faith-sparking examples of people doing crazy things because of faith. In a chapter called the faith chapter, you wouldn't expect to see anything about challenges, right? Or would you? The first couple of verses provide us with a definition as to what faith is. Following that definition are the real-life biblical examples of the real people that accomplished really big things through their unshakable faith in God. It's seriously inspiring to see a summary of just some of the things that God has accomplished through people who were willing to step out and do something uncomfortable. The author of Hebrews gives over fifteen examples of epic faith. Looking at this chapter through our handy-dandy through filter, something jumps out that otherwise can be easily overshadowed by the faith stories. Smack-dab in the middle of the list of faith acts are verses thirteen through seventeen:

> All these people died still believing what God
> had promised them. They did not receive what

was promised, but they saw it all from a distance and welcomed it. They agreed that they were foreigners and nomads here on earth. Obviously, people who say such things are looking forward to a country they can call their own. If they had longed for the country they came from, they could have gone back. But they were looking for a better place, a heavenly homeland. That is why God is not ashamed to be called their God, for He has prepared a city for them. (Hebrews 11:13–17)

This scripture holds the key to which these individuals were able to shift their perspectives of the storms they encountered and went through. This scripture holds a key that we too can begin to apply to our own struggles and storms. These people were looking for a better place, a heavenly homeland. Did you catch it? Their minds were fixed solely on heaven. When heaven becomes a reality to us, it drastically helps us along in our own through journeys. Whether it was Paul, Peter, or any of the individuals listed out in Hebrews 11, life with God, after life on this earth, was a reality to them. They lived their lives on a mission and viewed their daily activities as investments into their lives after this one. Heaven was also a very evident and real aspect of Jesus's life here on earth. Jesus had a different perspective than anyone else at that time. Me and you, we are humans. As humans here on earth, we have a linear, progressive perspective, earth to heaven. Jesus was the opposite. He came down to the earth He created. Jesus had a heaven to earth perspective. This changed everything. He knew where He came from and where He was going. That being the case, you might be thinking, *Well, no wonder it was possible for Jesus to go through things. He knew about the reality of heaven.* Of course, having the opportunity to actually go to heaven while we are still here on earth would be epic, but for the majority of us who don't get to experience that, we must continue to allow the reality of God's Spirit in us to build up and produce faith for that coming day. Jesus came to bring heaven to earth.

After Jesus rose from the dead, he appeared to all His disciples. All the disciples were locked in a room together, afraid for their lives after witnessing the brutal murder of their teacher. All were there, except one of them, Thomas. Dang it, Thomas. I can't blame him though. If I just saw one of my best friends murdered, and their murderers are still out there, and I knew that they also didn't like me because of my association with him, I might not be too eager to go outside. You know, there are a lot of instances throughout the gospels that I really relate with how Thomas responded to things. Ironically, Thomas' nickname was the twin. So often, his responses to things were basically a mirror image of things that humanity would do if placed in the same scenario. Ah, my twin, Thomas. So when Jesus appeared to His disciples after He rose from the grave, they were all there except for Thomas. Of course, after the disciples saw their resurrected rabbi, they freaked out and had to tell Thomas. Thomas, being the twin of humanity, instead of responding with faith and joy, said something along the lines of, "Okay, sure. Y'all are crazy. I'll need to see it to believe it." I can't even tell you how many times I've responded to things as a skeptic instead of responding in faith. About a week later, the disciples gathered together again. Only this time, they were able to convince Thomas to come out to be with them. While they were together, Jesus showed up yet again. In classic Jesus fashion, He used this as a teaching moment with Thomas, which we can still apply to our lives today.

> You believe because you have seen me. Blessed are those who believe without seeing me. (John 20:29)

A beautiful component to our lives here on earth are the unseen realities. Sure, Jesus saw with His very eyes the reality of heaven. That, no doubt, affected His perspective while here on earth. But we too have the opportunity to see heaven in our hearts. My point in saying all this is that even though we haven't seen heaven with our two eyes, through faith, we can still embrace its reality and allow that reality to shape our daily perspective. Eternity is real. Heaven is real.

I believe this to be true. Sure, I haven't personally been to heaven, but my life has genuinely been changed by God. Who I am today is NOT who I was before Jesus. The more we read the Word of God, the more we get an understanding of God's character. The more we learn what the Bible says, the more promises we are able to hold on to. Here are some promises regarding heaven, eternity, and how it can affect our lives here on earth:

> For I fully expect and hope that I will never be ashamed, but that I will continue to be bold for Christ, as I have been in the past. And I trust that my life will bring honor to Christ, whether I live or die. For to me, living means living for Christ, and dying is even better. But If I live, I can do more fruitful work for Christ. So I really don't know which is better. I'm torn between two desires: I long to go and be with Christ, which would be far better for me. But for your sakes, it is better than I continue to live. (Philippians 1:20–23)

> Above all, you must live as citizens of Heaven, conducting yourselves in a manner worthy of the Good News about Christ… (Philippians 1:27)

> For we know that when this earthly tent we live in is taken down (that is, when we die and leave this earthly body), we will have a house in Heaven, an eternal body made for us by God Himself and not by human hands. (2 Corinthians 5:1)

> So, we are always confident, even though we know that as long as we live in these bodies we are not at home with the Lord. For we live by believing and not by seeing. Yes, we are fully confident, and we would rather be away from these

earthly bodies, for then we will be at home with
the Lord." (2 Corinthians 5:6–8)

Since you have been raised to new life with
Christ, <u>set your sights on the realities of Heaven</u>,
where Christ sits in the place of honor at God's
right hand. <u>Think about the things of Heaven</u>,
not the things of Earth. For you died to this life,
and your real life is hidden with Christ in God.
(Colossians 3:1–2)

It's EVERYWHERE. Once you add this filter to your views, it's
impossible to ignore. This is a mind-set flip, a complete paradigm
shift. These passages of scripture can change everything about the
way you view hardships. Does it make it less painful? Absolutely not.
But what it does produce is purpose from the pain, hope that sur-
passes reason, and endurance that will get you through to the other
side. The more you allow yourself to go through your hardships,
the more God works in you and through you. What if instead of
running away from our problems, we embraced them as a normal
part of this temporary life here on earth, invite God into it with
us, and allow Him to use it to strengthen us and change the world
around us? These individuals knew that if they wanted to experience
God's strength to the fullest extent, they would need to embrace their
weaknesses. What if the pathway to true, genuine strength is paved
with pain and suffering? We see this time and time again in the Bible.
What if the storms are necessary to shape us into the best versions of
ourselves? What if we attempt to avoid going through the very thing
that is going to propel us forward in life?

James 1:1–4 says, "My fellow believers, when it seems as though
you are facing nothing but difficulties, see it as an invaluable opportunity to experience the greatest joy that you can! For you know
that when your faith is tested it stirs up power within you to endure
all things. And then as your endurance grows even stronger, it will
release perfection into every part of your being until there is nothing
missing and nothing lacking."

God, help us to see purpose in our pain. Help us to not blame you for the bad things that happen in our lives. You don't cause them to us. They are a result of the sinful world that we temporarily live in. Help us to have a heavenly perspective. Help us to look forward to our heavenly homeland. The next time you discover a leak in your roof that was caused by a storm (literally or metaphorically), instead of trying to ignore it, fix it yourself, or get upset because it happened, try to shift your perspective. Allow thankfulness to well up in your soul. I'm not saying that the leak isn't extremely irritating, inconvenient, and frustrating. Oh, believe me, I know it is. All I'm saying is that sometimes in life, the storms we try to avoid are the very things that show us the areas in our lives that we need Jesus's healing in the most. Before moving any further in this book, take some time to reflect. Think about some leaks in your ceiling. Once you've listed out a few, I'm going to challenge you to invite God into your house and ask Him to begin the patching process. Storms in life quickly reveal the cracks in our hearts. Rather than trying to patch them up ourselves with duct tape, invite the master carpenter in to do a deep healing. If the thought of prayer intimidates you or you're not sure where to start, I'll give you an example that you can follow along with and read out loud.

"Father, you are good. No matter what I feel, no matter what I see, I choose to say that You are good. I invite you into my heart. I surrender (insert cracks here) to you. Thank you for hearing me. Thank you for caring about the details of my life. I love you. Amen."

5

DON'T FORGET TO PACK AN ANCHOR

Do you have someone in your life that is a professional packer? You know what I'm talking about. The supermom that has literally EVERYTHING in their purse—bandages, Neosporin, cereal bars, cereal boxes, screwdrivers, hammers. You need it? They got it. It's CRAZY how they fit everything in there. My mom is like that. Whatever you need, whenever you need it, she pulls it out of thin air. Karen and I call this phenomenon Momazon. Clever, I know. It's insane how prepared some people are. I feel unprepared for most things in life. Not because I don't care about being prepared. I usually just wait until the last minute to do things, and inevitably, I forget things. One thing that I despise the most in the planning realm is packing a suitcase. I love the concept of traveling, but the whole process of traveling is more undesirable to me than having dandruff. I love being places. I just hate getting there. I'd rather spend the afternoon getting a cavity drilled than to be squeezed in the middle seat of an airplane for four-plus hours. Karen dislikes the middle seat, so being the selfless husband that I am, she either gets the aisle or the window if it's available. The middle seat is my seat. I get uncomfortable just thinking about it. There was one time that Karen and I went to New York for the Hillsong Conference there. It was SUCH an incredible experience. The middle seat was well worth it. We not only had the opportunity to attend the conference. We made a little vacation out of it with Karen's family from Guatemala as well. We met them there a couple of days before the conference and stayed a couple of days after. By doing this, it gave us enough time to adventure around the city. If you haven't had the opportunity to visit New York, I highly encourage you to make an effort to do so at some point in your life. The food is incredible, the culture is rich, and it's just flat-out cool. We were there for about eight days in total. When we neared the fifth or sixth day, I encountered a personal problem. In the morning, when I was preparing my outfit for the day, I realized that I only had one more pair of boxers. Of COURSE, I didn't pack enough underwear for the trip. You'd think that by now, after thirty years of life, I would learn to pack before midnight the night prior to our flight. Maybe someday. Here's the dilemma I was faced with in our tiny little Brooklyn Airbnb. Do I rewear the pairs of underwear I have? You know, do the flipperoo trick or find a place to buy them and spend the money that we had budgeted for souvenirs. Talk about a nice souvenir: fruit of the loom from New York. Needless to say, with Karen's help and input, we decided to go sightseeing at the Target down the street and purchase some undies. What I will tell you next is quite possibly irony in its purest form. They didn't even have my size in underwear. For real? It was either going to be too big or too small. Not sure what you would have done in the same situation, but I opted for the smaller pairs. I don't know. Something about having large underwear in New York when it's hot and humid outside, and you're walking everywhere, and it begins riding up… Okay, I'll stop there. Please pray for me. I'm not sure if that experience completely changed my packing habits, but what I can say is that for summer camp a few months after that, I definitely did NOT forget to pack enough underwear.

I think preparation and planning are two things that are such a vital aspect of our lives. If you fail to plan, you plan to fail. In the previous chapter, we learned that storms are a part of all our lives. It's not a matter of *if* a storm will come. It's a matter of *when* a storm will come. The question you must pause and ask yourself now is, "Am I prepared for when the storm hits?" Knowing that a storm is coming can encourage us to do our part to make sure we are safe physically, spiritually, and emotionally when it does. If you're reading this in the middle of a storm now, don't worry. It's never too late to begin your preparations. Preparation at any point in the storm will greatly reduce the amount of collateral damage the storm can cause.

From my personal perspective, it seems as though our culture thrives on impulsive reactions rather than responses. My dad is a professional planner. He always has toilet paper and paper towels in stock at his house. My stepmom, on the other hand, always gives him a hard time when he wants to buy more paper towels from Costco, even though they already have a surplus of them. Why not buy a pack of thirty paper towels? Who can resist? When the year 2020 hit, the entire world was faced with the global pandemic of COVID-19. Because of the outbreak of coronavirus, people from all around the world were quarantined to their homes to slow the spread of the virus. This is something unlike anything we've ever seen in our lifetimes. When the news from the government came and ordered everyone to stay inside, safer at home, people literally FREAKED out. This was the moment that all the planners and doomsday preparers have been waiting for their entire lives. There are a lot of things from this season that I'll honestly never forget. The need to wear masks whenever in public, the hyperawareness of washing our hands and touching our faces, the shock of seeing the shelves at grocery stores and department stores completely bare, learning how to do literally everything online, how to make yourself a potato on Zoom meetings, and so much more. There is one thing in particular from this whole quarantine experience that I will never fully understand. Why is it that when people were freaking out and panic buying things from the stores once quarantine started, they bought SO MUCH TOILET PAPER? It's like people were more concerned about stocking up on toilet paper than food and water. Look, if you need twenty rolls of toilet paper to get you through a couple weeks of being at home, you needed to have a doctor to check you out even before the whole COVID pandemic. Can't blame people for wanting to be prepared though.

I believe with my whole heart that God not only wants us to survive storms. He wants us to thrive in storms. He wants us to come out on the other side of the storm stronger than we were when the storm began. He wants us to show that storm who's boss. He doesn't want us to be caught off guard by the storms. If you're expecting the storm, you can work it. God is like, in theory, our heavenly weatherman. He uses His Word to give us a forecast, letting us know that our lives here on earth have rainy days. Now of course, it would be nice to know WHEN those rainy days will come. Like, I can look at the weekly forecast and see, hmm, I'm going to find out on Friday that my cousin has an eating disorder. Or like, in mine and Karen's case, on Monday we will get the news that our baby passed away. Unfortunately, that's not the way life works. So knowing that hard days are a part of life, we can do our best to prepare before they come. Have you ever seen those videos of those crazy surfers who surf during storms? They actually plan for and look FORWARD to storms. They create the gnarliest tubes bra. I want to be that type of Christian. I want to rock the storm. In order for us to thrive in storms, we must be prepared for when it comes.

> Take a lesson from the ants, you lazybones. Learn from their ways and become wise! Though they have no prince or governor or ruler to make them work, they labor hard all summer, gathering food for the winter. But you, lazybones, how long will you sleep? (Proverbs 6:6–8)

When you have good days, prepare. When you have nice moments, prepare. When you have sunny skies, start to store up things. Don't wait until the storm hits to start getting ready for it. Now that we've talked about the importance of preparation, let's talk about *how* to prepare. You don't want to be that one Californian that decides to go to the grocery store in the middle of a storm and then realizes they forgot their umbrella at home as soon as they pull into the parking lot, do you? Let's get prepared.

If you've ever been camping, you know the importance of preparation. Here's the thing with packing for camping though. I've never planned a camping trip in my life. I don't even know where to begin when it comes to knowing what to pack. The best people to help you pack for a camping trip are those who have been camping many times before. They can tell you what kind of things you will encounter and what kind of things you will need to pack in order to respond to those particular things well. When it comes to learning how to prepare for going through pain in life, it's imperative that you learn how to pack from someone that's been there before. What I want to do in this next part of the book is learn how to pack from someone that has been through some serious storms in life.

King David was a man that was highly acquainted with going through storms. He knew what pain felt like. Reading through the book of Psalms is like getting a sneak peek into David's personal journal. Though not all the psalms are acquitted to King David's authorship, a majority of them are. Psalms are simply songs or melodies. When we read through the songs of Psalms, we see songs of praise, adoration, thankfulness, and gratitude. On the other hand, we also see psalms of pain, suffering, repentance, and pleas for forgiveness. When you understand the life of King David and the difficulties he went through, you can better understand the songs he writes and how easily they can be applied to our pain as well.

Early on in David's life, Saul, the first king of Israel, invited David into his court because of David's ability to play the harp. Yet after David fought and killed a giant named Goliath in battle, Saul grew extremely jealous over David's growing popularity. In fact, Saul became so jealous of David that he began to plot ways of killing him. From this time until the very end of his life, Saul made it his personal mission to kill David. As a result of this, David was chased around the region and forced into isolation, and many were turned against him. Though there are many hardships that we can read about in King David's life, which come as a result of poor decisions he made, being hunted down by Saul was thrust upon him. It was completely outside his control. Throughout the various psalms that David wrote, we get a glimpse into triumph, victory, and freedom, but also, we get to see genuine heartbreak, brokenness, doubt, depression, and even fear. If King David, a man after God's own heart as the Bible describes him, goes through brokenness, why should it come as a surprise when we go through it too? Here are a few songs that give us insight into just how broken, alone, and forgotten David felt at times:

> I am worn out from sobbing. All night I flood my bed with weeping, drenching it with my tears. My vision is blurred by grief; my eyes are worn out because of all my enemies. (Psalm 6:6–7)

> Have mercy on me, Lord, for I am in distress. Tears blur my eyes. My body and soul are withering away. I am dying from grief; my years are shortened by sadness. Sin has drained my strength; I am wasting away from within. I am scorned by all my enemies and despised by my neighbors—even my friends are afraid to come near me. When they see me on the street, they run the other way. I am ignored as if I were dead, as if I were a broken pot. I have heard the many rumors about me, and I am surrounded by terror. My enemies conspire against me, plotting to take my life." (Psalm 31:9–13)

> My God, my God, why have you abandoned me? Why are you so far away when I groan for help? Every day I call to you, my God, but You do not answer. Every night I lift my voice, but I find no relief. (Psalm 22:1–2)

Starting to see the Bible as relevant to your life? Starting to feel that you're not alone? I hope so. The book of Psalms has a very special place in my heart. Fun fact: Psalm 91 was actually the first piece of

Bible that I actually understood. Before I even knew how to read the Bible, I was given a printed 8.5 x 11 piece of paper that had Psalm 91 on it. I would read it every night before I went to bed. The Psalms are RICH, and if you've never read through them, I highly encourage you to do so. These types of psalms, the psalms that I listed above, are referred to as psalms of lament. To lament is to simply express grief or sorrow in a passionate manner. Sometimes, you just have to LET IT OUT. King David knew how to let it out. Releasing your hurt and pain is actually one of the healthiest ways to begin the healing process. If you go through something traumatic and never talk about it to anyone, you can actually cause damage to your brain. As if 2019 wasn't challenging enough, in the concluding months, a shooting took place at a local school where Karen and I live. The news stories that you read and see that cover shootings are absolutely devastating, but when it happens in your city, to people that you personally know, it hits home on a whole new level. As a youth pastor with students that were directly affected, I asked a therapist how I should respond. I didn't know if I should do a teaching on a specific subject or what. Her response to me was "Get the kids comfortable, and get them talking." A sermon isn't going to help them heal in that moment. The right words won't even come close to fixing what happened. Get them talking. We got them into small groups on a Sunday morning and just encouraged them to open up dialogue with each other. By doing this, getting the students to talk, it actually rid their bodies of toxins that could build up because of the trauma. If we don't talk through our storms for fear of burdening others or rejection, toxins can actually begin to build up in our brain and eventually cause our brains to shut down. It's always been so hard for me to express myself and talk through my problems. I don't really know why, but I had this subconscious fear that I was burdening people, that my problems weren't going to be a big deal to them. This kind of mind-set led to me experiencing a mental breakdown a couple months after we lost Asher. I didn't know how to let it out.

In April 2019, I started to experience things physically that I'd never experienced before. The first time that I was aware of what was happening, I was drumming in a Sunday service at our church. All throughout the sound check, I was fine. When the first song of the first Sunday service began, my heart started racing. I started to feel light-headed, my fingers started to tingle, I got really dizzy, and my vision started going to a tunnel. I thought I was having a heart attack. I pushed through it, barely, and right as we concluded worship of that service, I went in the side room and just sat on a couch there. I didn't know what was happening at the time. This was the first of many panic attacks that I experienced in this season of my life. Every time I was asked to drum at church, I felt the same thing. It started off just happening while drumming, but shortly after, that same feeling started to bleed into when I was driving. I couldn't even be in the car for more than twenty minutes before feeling like I was going to pass out. There were multiple times where I had to pull off into a parking lot to just calm myself down. This kept happening and eventually hit a climax when Karen and I traveled to Nashville, Tennessee, for a church conference. While there in Nashville, I couldn't even relax. The whole time, I was consumed with fear for my life. I had no appetite, no drive, and no focus. My senses were on constant high alert. When the music was too loud, I started to panic. When I was simply walking down the hall and I felt a slight shift in the floor or it began to calmly shake because of the elevator, I started to panic. I couldn't rest. On one of the free nights we had at the conference, we had the opportunity to sit down with two friends of ours and get some sushi. This conversation changed my life. I don't recall exactly how it came up in our conversation, but it did. I started to share with them what I was feeling. Sure enough, one of our friends had battled through the very same thing I was going through. She had been through that storm. From that conversation, I was introduced to the idea of going to therapy. She recommended a therapist that had helped her through her anxiety and depression and was confident she'd do the same for me. At first, I was hesitant because remember, I have a hard time talking about my problems. Therapy is TALKING. Let me tell you, I'm so glad that I did. That therapist was an absolute godsend. She helped me learn that I'm not going crazy and that the pain I was feeling was completely normal due to the things I went through. I'm not sure what your opinion of therapy is, but from someone that has been helped immensely from it, I highly recommend it. Having a trained professional explain to you what's happening physically and emotionally to you is truly so healing. It doesn't disregard the Bible. In fact, I've learned so much about God's intricate design of our bodies through therapy. It's incredible. I learned the beauty of letting it out.

The psalms that David wrote were his way of letting it out. The psalms are all so different, yet a lot of them have a similar pattern. The outline goes something like this: opening, complaint, request, and expression of trust. The expression of trust has always been something that inspired me about David's heart. It didn't matter how down he was. He always expressed faith and hope in God. Psalm 13 is a psalm that has easily become one of my favorite chapters in all of the Bible. It goes like this:

> O Lord, how long will you forget me? Forever? How long will you look the other way? How long must I struggle with anguish in my soul, with sorrow in my heart every day? How long will my enemy have the upper hand? Turn and answer me, O Lord my God! Restore the sparkle to my eyes, or I will die. Don't let my enemies gloat, saying, "we have defeated him!" Don't let them rejoice at my downfall. (Psalm 13:1–4)

Pretty intense, right? There is so much about this part of the chapter that I relate with. There are so many times when I've felt forgotten. There are times when I've felt ignored and passed over. There are days when I've felt as though the anguish in my soul would never go away. There are moments when I simply just want to give up. But David's psalm doesn't end here. This is where it gets good. He goes on to say the following verses:

> But I trust in your unfailing love. I will rejoice because you have rescued me. I will sing to the Lord because He is good to me. (Psalm 13:5–6)

Every time I read this chapter, I get so fired up. It's so real, it's so raw, and it's so relatable in so many ways. David is expressing his internal struggle, a struggle very similar to ones that we too experience. In the middle of his storm, he drops a big, faith-filled *but*. King David has a big *but*. We need bigger *buts*. No matter what he was feeling, he CHOSE to trust God. The *but* is acknowledging the pain BUT choosing to trust God. No matter how big the problem was, King David busted out the big *but*. The word *trust* from Psalm 13:5 derives from a phrase that means choosing to be bold, secure, and undaunted. Trust is a choice. It goes beyond what we feel. The key to trust, which is so evident in King David's life, is to personally know God and understand the promises He has for you in His Word.

Psalm 18 is an absolutely beautiful psalm. David wrote this particular song on the day that God rescued him from Saul's attacks on him. David was in the middle of a storm. When you read through this, watch out for three things: how intimately David knew God, how he acknowledged his pain and didn't run from it, and how he held on to God's promises:

> I love You, Lord; You are my strength. The Lord is my rock, my fortress, and my savior; my God is my rock, in whom I find protection. He is my shield, the power that saves me, and my place of safety. I called on the Lord, who is worthy of praise, and He saved me from my enemies. The ropes of death entangled me; floods of destruction swept over me. The grave wrapped its ropes around me; death laid a trap in my path. But in my distress, I cried out to the Lord; yes, I prayed to my God for help. He heard me from His sanctuary; my cry to Him reached His ears. The earth quaked and trembled. The foundations of the mountains shook; they quaked and trembled. The foundations of the mountains shook; they quaked because of His anger... To the pure You

show yourself pure, but to the crooked You show yourself shrewd. You rescue the humble, but You humiliate the proud. You light a lamp for me. The Lord, my God, lights up my darkness. In Your strength I can crush an army; with my God I can scale any wall. God's way is perfect. All the Lord's promises prove true. He is a shield for all who look to Him for protection. (Psalm 18:1–7, 26–30)

King David was able to quote and hold on to God's promises. No matter how difficult the situation appeared, no matter how dire the outcome seemed, David knew God's promises, and he knew that God always kept His word. Because God always keeps His word, David was able to face anything. The more time we spend in God's Word, the more familiar we become with the promises He makes to us. The more familiar we are with the promises that God makes to us, the more secure our hope becomes. God wants you to have hope. That's why He gave us the Bible. David had an intimate relationship with God. Look at what he says in his psalm below:

And so, Lord, where do I put my hope? My only hope is in You. (Psalm 39:7)

Because David knew God's promises, he had hope. Because he had hope, he was anchored, no matter how intense the storms of life became. He knew that no matter how hard the wind was blowing, no matter how torrential the downpour was, he would still be standing firm when the storm stopped.

I want to show you this passage of scripture out of Hebrews 6 that illustrates this concept of God's promises and hope in a beautiful way:

For example, there was God's promise to Abraham. Since there was no one greater to swear by, God took an oath in His own name, saying: "I will certainly bless you, and I will multiply your descendants beyond number." Then Abraham waited patiently, and he received what God had promised. Now when people take an oath, they call on someone greater than themselves to hold them to it. And without any question that oath is binding. God also bound Himself with an oath, so that those who received the promise could be perfectly sure that He would never change His mind. So God has given both His promise and His oath. These two things are unchangeable because it is impossible for God to lie. Therefore, we who have fled to Him for refuge can have great confidence as we hold to the hope that lies before us. This hope is a strong and trustworthy anchor for our souls. It leads us through the curtain into God's inner sanctuary. (Hebrews 6:13–19)

I absolutely love how the Bible describes hope as an anchor for our souls. Your soul is defined as your mind, will, and emotions. Simply put, your soul is how healthy your thought life is, how motivated you are, and how your heart is emotionally. It's the inner you. Knowing God's promises safeguards the health of our soul. Let's really dig apart this idea of God's promise to being an anchor. What does an anchor do? Does it prevent storms from happening? No. Does it make sure that the boat isn't affected by the wind and waves? No. An anchor's job is to ensure that the boat won't drift away from its intended location once the wind and waves come. When you're anchored, it doesn't mean that you won't get a little rocked from the waves that bombard you. What it does mean is that when the storm has finally subsided, you will be standing firm in your soul. You won't be miles off where you were before the storm came. I have to be honest. I don't have any clue how people make it through losing a child, or losing anyone for that matter, without the hope of eternity. It's that hope—that hope that's rooted in God's promises in His Word—that sustained me and Karen when the storm of 2019 hit us. I knew deep down that no matter how difficult and confusing the whole loss was, there would be a day that Karen and I held Asher in heaven. It's no wonder to me that people get mad at God and walk away from Him and the church when wind and waves come. If there isn't an anchor to keep you grounded, those waves can take you far from where you desire to be. It's so important that we build our lives on the foundation of God's Word. Jesus gives us this example in Matthew 7:

> Anyone who listens to my teaching and follows it is wise, like a person who builds a house on solid rock. Though the rain comes in torrents and the floodwaters rise and the winds beat against that house, it won't collapse because it is built on bedrock. But anyone who hears my teaching and doesn't obey it is foolish, like a person who builds a house on sand. When the rains and floods come and the winds beat against that house, it will collapse with a mighty crash. (Matthew 7:24–27)

Notice again how the scripture says *when* and not *if* rains and floods come. I don't know about you, but I want to build my life on a bedrock. I want to be standing firm after the storms of life hit. I want to be prepared for this!

To be anchored in God's Word means to be rooted in Him. The healthier your root system is, the stronger you remain through storms. So often, the Bible compares and contrasts our relationships with God to plants.

> Let your roots grow down into Him, and let your lives be built on Him. Then your faith will grow strong in the truth you were taught, and you will overflow with thankfulness. (Colossians 2:7)

Recently, I've grown a deeper appreciation for plants. When Karen and I first got married, she developed a love for growing and planting a wide variety of plants in our apartment. I didn't really develop an appreciation for it until recently, when we ventured into the world of propagation. If you don't know what that means, I don't blame you. Propagation is the process of cutting pieces off from healthy plants that you already have and replanting them to make another plant. We have a couple of different types of succulents that started to outgrow their pots. Karen discovered that there's a way to cut pieces of the succulent off and replant them. Rather than just cutting it off and sticking it into some dirt, which is probably what I would have done, you need to set the cut pieces in some water until it begins to grow roots. It's a fascinating process watching the succulents growing roots. Once the roots get to a certain length, then you can plant it into a pot with dirt in it. Having healthy roots is vital to a healthy life for the plants. So it is the same for us as humans in this life that we've been given to live. The roots are an anchoring system for the plants, which not only hold them into place when storms come. They provide health and nutrients also. When you know God's Word, you know His promises for you. When you know His promises for you, your soul is anchored. When your soul is anchored, no storm will be able to overthrow you. No wind can take you away from God's path for you. You will not only still be standing once the storm passes, but you will be so much stronger than you were before it came. I challenge you, with anything that you're facing right now, whether it's fear for tomorrow, feeling unloved, feeling unworthy, search what the Bible says about that. Write out some specific scriptures that combat that specific things you're fighting against, and watch as those words anchor your soul. The situation might not change immediately, but your outlook of that situation will, and that's everything. If we are healthy on the inside, it doesn't matter what hits us on the outside. We will still be standing. The more prepared you are, the better.

Don't forget to pack an anchor.

6

THE SUN WILL COME
OUT TOMORROW

Storms come in many different shapes and sizes. To one, a storm can be losing a loved one. To another, a storm can be finding out that your husband or wife has been cheating on you. To another, it's missing out on a job opportunity that you've been preparing years for. To another, it's getting broken up with by the person you thought you'd spend the rest of your life with. To another, it's saying goodbye to your dog that has been by your side for twelve years. To another, it can be getting made fun of at school. No matter the duration, intensity, or frequency, a storm is a storm. Here's a beautiful truth to hold on to in regards to storms though: the sun will always come out tomorrow. Maybe the sun won't break through for a week, month, or even years, but the sun WILL shine again. You can bet your bottom dollar.

Have you ever been on an airplane? It took me until I was twenty-one to get on my first flight. It was from Los Angeles to Alabama. I'll never forget that feeling of excitement welling up within my stomach before the first takeoff. I had no idea what to expect. It was exhilarating. I remember sitting in the middle seat (like always), seat belt fashioned beyond securely, clenching for dear life to the armrests, and bracing myself for anything that could happen. Fun fact about Brandon: I always think of the worst possible scenario that could happen, no matter what I'm doing. Some say that it's a great survival instinct. I think it's exhausting. You hear the announcements chime on all the personal screens at once, telling you about how to survive if oxygen levels drop or the plane crashes into water. You know, normal flying things. Then before you know it, the pilot's voice comes over the speakers: "Prepare for takeoff." The engines go into overdrive, the plane peels down the runway, and you are pinned to the back of your seat as the plane takes off into the open sky.

Being married to someone from another country means dating someone from another country before you get married. Dating someone from another country means traveling to another country by means of the air multiple times a year. You'd think that I would be used to it by now, right? Wrong. I still don't trust the idea of flying superfast, superhigh, and superlong by someone I've never met. I have trust issues. I envy the people that can sleep on flights. What I would give to be able to do that. No matter how many sleep aids I take, no matter how little I slept the night before, my body never rests enough on a plane to go to sleep. Turbulence, don't even get me started. I'll never forget this one time I was flying back to Los Angeles from Guatemala. I thought it was going to be the end for me. While we were driving to the airport, it started raining. Like, really raining. Guatemala rain. By the time we got to the airport, the rain had subsided, but looking up into the clouds, I began to see lightning bolts shoot through the distant sky. It was nice knowing you. Now, normally when I fly, I think I'm more stressed out than the average traveler. This time in particular was a whole new level of freak-out. Gotta play it cool though, you know? Can't let the girlfriend know I'm freaking out. I think I hugged her for ten minutes before letting go. Before I knew it, I was in my chair, seat belt fastened tightly, ready to take off to my demise. I didn't even have my own screen! Don't you hate when you don't have your own personal screen on a flight? The safety videos played, the flight attendants walked the aisles checking the luggage and seat belts, and then, without warning, the plane started to take off. I THOUGHT THE PILOT GAVE A WARNING. Not this time. I closed my eyes as the plane's wheels began to lift off of the runway. I felt the G-Force push me back like usual, and I was halfway expecting a lightning bolt to SHOCK the plane. I looked out the window and saw as the plane approached the dark clouds. Here it comes. This is it. I even see a lightning bolt in the distance. The plane goes dark because we are now passing through the cloud. It begins to shake because of the shift in temperatures and pressures of the outside air. I took a deep breath, bracing myself for the inevitable, and before I knew it. *Boom!* Beams of sunlight shot into the cabin of the plane. Believe me, I was as shocked as you are now. Let me also add that I would have, FOR SURE, had the windows closed for takeoff, but for whatever reason, they make you keep it open. I'm sure there's a logical explanation for the torture. I just don't know it. The sun burst into the plane, warming everything it touched. Just thirty seconds before that, I was in a literal storm. Thunder clouds, rain, dark clouds, the whole nine yards. In an instant, the plane burst above the clouds and was smoothly flying at the cruising altitude. I looked out the window and saw the dark clouds underneath us with nothing but clear skies and sun ahead. I knew in that moment that everything was going to be okay. I knew I was going to make it home.

It's so easy to forget about the clear skies that sit above the gloomy clouds when you're in the middle of a storm. But I have to be honest with you. Ever since I had that experience, I will never forget that the storms we face, literal and metaphorical, will pass too. There will be a day that the sun comes out again. No matter how dark the clouds are, the sun hasn't gone anywhere. It might not be visible to you at the moment, but it's only a matter of time until it breaks through again. When clouds are blocking out the sun, it truly does take faith to know that the sun is still there, even if you can't see it or feel its warmth.

Something I hope this book does for you is encourage you that you will make it to the other side of your storm. There's something encouraging about knowing that someone has been through the very same thing you're going through. Reading through the Bible, it seems as though storms didn't really faze Jesus. Jesus had his fair share of storms to go through. There's a story in Matthew 8 when He and His disciples encountered a sudden and abrupt storm.

> As evening came, Jesus said to His disciples, "Let's cross to the other side of the lake." So, they took Jesus in the boat and started out, leaving the crowds behind (although other boats followed). But soon a fierce storm came up. High waves were breaking into the boat, and it began to fill with water. Jesus was sleeping at the back of the boat with His head on a cushion. The disciples woke Him up, shouting, "Teacher, don't you care that we're going to drown?" When Jesus woke up, He rebuked the wind and said to the waves, "Silence! Be still!" Suddenly the wind stopped, and there was a great calm. (Mark 4:35–39)

Think about this for a second from the disciples' perspective. Jesus tells you to get into a boat to cross a lake. In the middle of that journey, you start to get rocked by a violent storm. Jesus, the Son of God, seemingly led them into danger. Have you ever felt that God has done that to you? Not only did Jesus seemingly lead them into a storm. He was ASLEEP! The disciples begin to freak out for their lives, and Jesus is snuggled up, snoozing. The Bible even mentions that He had His head on a cushion. Not only is God ignoring my problems. He's comfortable doing so! Have you ever felt, like the disciples did, that Jesus didn't care about the storm that you were in? Have you ever felt like God was sleeping on your requests? Can I tell you that there is no storm that we go through that God doesn't care about? Following Jesus again doesn't mean there will be no storms. Jesus knew that He was going to encounter storms. I'm convinced that nothing took Him by surprise. Greater than His fear of the storm though was His belief in the truth that His Father had a plan for His life. A plan that was unshakable by the things that tried to hit it over. He knew He was going to make it to the other side of that lake. Because Jesus knew that He was going to make it, He was able to literally sleep through the storm. Sleeping through the storm doesn't mean that Jesus doesn't care about the storm. He could have easily shrugged off the disciples' fear-stricken request and told them to suck it up. He woke up, rebuked the wind and waves, and used it as a teaching moment for the disciples about having faith in God. There is a significant shift that takes place internally once we truly begin to believe that God has a plan for our lives. Jesus knew that His Father had a plan for His life, and no storm was going to prevent that from coming to pass. When we too begin to believe that God has a purpose for our lives, we begin to shift our focus beyond the wind and waves. By shifting our focus, we open ourselves up to an inner peace that can allow sweet sleep even in the midst of violent storms. I want to encourage you, my friend. If you're reading these words, there is more for your life. God has every day of your life mapped out, and trust me, it's the greatest adventure of all time, beginning to discover exactly what that is.

God desires for you to have a vision for your life. Having a vision is simply believing that there is more—more to experience, more to learn, more to accomplish, more in store. Having a vision is knowing that what you've experienced up until this point in your life is only but a glimpse of what's to come. God wants you to dream. What's a desire that you have deep within your heart that seems impossible to accomplish? I urge you to tap into God-sized dreams. What fun is there in having dreams for your life that you can accomplish in and through your own strength? When the end of my time here on earth comes, I want to look back and see all that God accomplished in and through me. I don't want to reflect back and see things that I did in my own strength. May everything point back to Jesus and the reality of His presence in our lives. When we believe and hold on to anchors like Jeremiah 29:11 and Philippians 1:6, our focus shifts from problems to purpose. These scriptures say that God has good plans for us, plans that are good and are designed to give us a future and a hope for greater things. These scriptures promise us that God, who started a great work within us, will bring that to completion. His timing is greater than our timing. His thoughts are greater than our thoughts. These scriptures give us the anchors necessary to keep pressing forward in peace even when storms come.

Paul was definitely well-acquainted with storms, both literal and metaphorical. Remember how he was shipwrecked more than once? Toward the end of the book of Acts, there's a story of when Paul was nearly beaten to death by crowds of people who were outraged by the message he was preaching. He spoke the truth that God had called him to speak, and because of that, people were enraged. One instance, when Paul was being beat up by a crowd, Roman officials had been sent there to break up the commotion. When they realized that Paul was at the center of everything, they went in, arrested him, and brought him to a safe location for questioning. When the Roman officials were trying to figure out what he had done, they weren't able to because everyone was saying different things. In a private location, they even began to whip and beat Paul to try and get him to confess to what he did. In the midst of this, Paul mentioned that he was a Roman citizen by birth. Romans didn't treat other Romans like this. This type of brutality was a way that the Romans dealt with Jews. By making this claim, Paul was then to be transferred to Rome to make his plea of innocence before Caesar. While Paul was in captivity, before the trip to Rome, God called out to him and spoke purpose into his storm:

> That night the Lord appeared to Paul and said, "Be encouraged, Paul. Just as you have been a witness to me here in Jerusalem, you must preach the Good News in Rome as well." (Acts 23:11)

Paul knew that God was going to use this pain for a purpose. Paul knew God had gone before him and prepared a place for him to step into. The storm actually opened up a new opportunity for Paul to preach the gospel to a group of people who had never heard it before. The thing that amazes me about reading through the accounts of the early church in the book of Acts is how, whenever a problem or altercation rose up, they always used it as an opportunity to preach about Jesus. If they were in prison, they preached. If they were on trial or persecuted, they preached. Nothing could stop them from sharing about Jesus. There was never a victim mentality that developed because of the hardships they endured. They truly looked at everything that happened to them as unique opportunities to speak about God's goodness. There's a purpose in everything.

While Paul was on his way to Rome for his appeal, they got hit with a nasty storm. It's actually pretty comical reading through this story and paying attention to how Paul responded to everything that was going down. Before they set sail on their voyage, Paul literally told them, "I don't think it's a good idea to set sail. There's a storm a brewin'." (This is my interpretation.) Because of the time of year that they were on their trip, it was extremely dangerous due to severe weather conditions. I've been in this situation (metaphorically) more times than I'd like to admit. Warning signs are all around, wise counsel has spoken, weather conditions are iffy, and I still move forward into the open sea. Completely blowing Paul off, they decided to set sail anyways. Paul, in the Bible, literally said, "I believe there is trouble ahead if we go on. Shipwreck, loss of cargo, and danger to our lives as well." Sure enough, while they were out at sea, they got hit, and they got hit hard. The wind, according to the Bible, was like that of a typhoon. This wasn't just your normal gust of wind. This is the type of wind that will literally destroy your freakin' boat. After the sailors battled the winds and waves for a while, they eventually gave up. Have you ever been in a storm that was so intense and you fought so hard and so long without any relief that you decide to just give up and let the wind take you where it may? I've definitely been there. Paul's storm lasted for days. It was so intense even that the Bible says it "blotted out the sun and stars until at last, all hope was gone" (Acts 27:20). Wow! How relatable is this? The storm is so bad you can't see the sun and stars. You've lost your sense of direction, and it causes you to give up hope. Let me clarify, everyone lost hope except for Paul. Remember, Paul knew that God had called him to accomplish something, and no stinkin' storm was going to prevent that from happening. He had a vision that projected beyond the storm. He had dreams that surpassed what he could accomplish in his own strength. He had faith that sustained him. He had hope that anchored him.

At the time that all hope was lost in the crew, Paul gathered everyone together for a little powwow and said, "Men, you should have listened to me in the first place and not left Crete. You would have avoided all this damage and loss."

He's practically rubbing it in their faces now. Time and place, Paul. Time and place.

> But take courage! None of you will lose your lives, even though the ship will go down. For last night an angel of the God to whom I belong and whom I serve stood beside me, and he said, "Don't be afraid, Paul, for you will surely stand trial before Caesar! What's more, God in His goodness has granted safety to everyone sailing with you." So take courage! For I believe God. It will be just as He said. But we will be shipwrecked on an island. (Acts 27:21–26)

Hey! Everything's going to be okay! We're going to make it! God spoke to me and told me so! Oh yeah, almost forgot to mention that we will be shipwrecked. Couldn't God have just let them get through the storm and keep the boat along with all their possessions? One thing I've noticed about storms in my own life is that they strip away things that aren't of God. Sometimes we need the storm to happen to get a much-needed cleansing. The Bible says that the things we've inherited by putting our faith in God are unshakable, which means that when we go through situations that shake us to the core, on the other side of it, the only things that are left standing are that of God. God truly is unshakable. He's the only source that is like that. Everything else, no matter how secure and strong they may seem, will get destroyed in the intense storms of life. Whenever storms come, they quickly show us what we can trust in and what we cannot trust in. No matter how strong you think your boat is, there's going to be a storm one day that takes you by surprise and shows you just how fragile a boat can be.

I hate being wet. Let me clarify, I hate being wet when I'm not supposed to be wet. I like showers, Jacuzzis, swimming pools, and the occasional water park. On second thought, scratch that. I don't really like water parks either. There was a time that I was at a water park in their lazy river. You know those rivers that just ebb and flow around the whole park? So there I was, floating and minding my own business, and suddenly I was attacked by three bandages floating through the murky water. Game over. No gracias. Being wet when I'm supposed to be dry is like one of my worst nightmares. Sweat? No thanks. If ever I get wet and it's cold outside, instant sickness. This is why I never go on Splash Mountain at Disneyland or Jurassic Park at Universal Studios. I have a very traumatic memory that has to do with getting wet at a theme park from when I was in the fourth grade. Normally, I wouldn't share this story openly, but seeing as though we're practically best friends now and you've read this much of the book without quitting, I'll tell you. We are literally going to new levels of trust and openness here. So like I said, this happened when I was in the fourth grade. I was a part of this after-school program called Sunshine, which took field trips every so often. Over summer break, we would take field trips to different places every week. We would go to places like the beach, the park, or Magic Mountain, but there was one trip that I was looking forward to the most. I was PUMPED to go to Knott's Berry Farm. Looking back, I'm not entirely sure why I was so excited to go. Roller coasters make me sick. I think I was excited to go there because I really liked their strawberry jelly. Anyways, at the beginning of summer, Sunshine gave us a calendar that listed out the different activities that we would be going to do, and Knott's Berry Farm was at the end. It's like all the anticipation and excitement built up for that trip. We get there, and it was as amazing as I had dreamed it of being. We went on rides, ate greasy food, and had the time of our lives. The very last ride we went on was the one with water. I don't recall if it was called the Log Jammer or Roarin' Rapids or something like that. You get the picture. We went on it, and sure enough, I get soaked. Have you noticed that there is usually one person on water rides that gets the most wet? That is ALWAYS me. I somehow always pick the seat that gets the most water. Doesn't matter if it's in the front of the boat or the back of the boat. The water will always find me. At the end of the ride, I was, of course, soaked, and we made our way back to the buses to go home. Before we exited the park, we stopped off at the bathrooms. Nothing is worse than having a bunch of elementary school students on a bus for two hours needing to go to the bathroom. When we made it to the bathroom nearest to the exit of the park, we noticed that there was a line outside the men's bathroom. The women's bathroom was fine, but for some reason, the men's bathroom was backed up. No pun intended. We waited in the line for about five to ten minutes then had to get back to the buses. I was about to get into the bathroom before I realized that my group was leaving. I could have risked getting left behind at the park, or I could just suck it up and try to survive the bus ride home. Needless to say, I definitely DID NOT want to be left at an amusement park before I was trusted with a cell phone. At the time of leaving Knott's, I was convinced I could hold it. Fifteen minutes into the bus ride, I quickly realized I could not. Every bump was torture. Have you ever had to go pee so bad you thought that your bladder was going to literally explode? I was past that point. I was suffering. People around me probably thought I was having an emotional breakdown in a row all to myself. About the time when I was convinced I was going to develop a bladder disease because of holding it too long, I had an epiphany. I was already wet because of that water ride. Friend, reading this next part might make you look at me differently. Before you cast judgment, remember the irrational decisions you made in elementary school, okay? I thought to myself, *I'm already wet. Why not just pee yourself?* I did just that. I let it all out. You'd think that someone dumped out their whole large cup of lemonade on the bus. Yes, I was the kid that peed himself on the bus back home from Knott's Berry Farm. Let me tell you, I'd do it again. Well, maybe not. I'd probably just speak up and say I needed to go really bad before getting on the bus. In hindsight, changes would have been made. But it makes a rather comical story now, right? Being wet when you don't want to be makes you

THE SUN WILL COME OUT TOMORROW

so uncomfortable. When you're uncomfortable, you are tempted to make decisions that are emotionally charged.

Can I encourage you right now? If you feel as though a storm has beat you up and soaked all the clothes you have, don't give up. Don't jump ship. No matter how uncomfortable you feel, no matter how tempting it is to bail out, ride it out. I promise it will be worth it. In Paul's shipwreck story on his way to Rome, there's an interesting point to pull from the scripture before we get to the actual shipwreck. In the verse below, we see how people are starting to react to the unavoidable shipwreck as it quickly approached:

> Then the sailors tried to abandon the ship; they lowered the lifeboat as though they were going to put out anchors from the front of the ship. But Paul said to the commanding officer and the soldiers, "You will all die unless the sailors stay aboard," So the soldiers cut the ropes to the lifeboat and let it drift away. (Acts 27:30–31)

How interesting that if the soldiers would have literally jumped ship, God's provision would have been lifted. I think it says something significant about someone when they decide to stay no matter how intense the storm is. I've seen that oftentimes, when people feel pressure or endangered, they try to run away from the thing that's causing the danger. How was Paul able to ride out the storm? Simple. He knew God had more in store for his life. Could it be that we take ourselves out of a position to receive God's blessing if we quit or run away? These sailors were about to let fear cause them to miss out on a miracle. I wonder if there are any miracles that I've missed out on in my life because I've allowed fear to drive me to a point of jumping off the ship. When we try to control outcomes, sometimes we make things worse. Anxiety was most gripping in my mind when I wouldn't give up control of the outcomes of my life. I felt like I needed to control everything because I subconsciously rationalized that if I could control it, I would be safe. This pressure of control developed an almost debilitating personal anxiety in me. Could it be that rather than jumping off the ship, we need to ride it out? What if the shipwreck is necessary to get rid of some nasty things we've built up in our lives? The shipwreck was going to happen, and Paul was urging everyone to stay on board. It's easy to start something but challenging to stay, especially when times get tough.

With the wind and waves beating relentlessly upon the boat, eventually it couldn't stand anymore. The ship broke apart in the violent waves, forcing all 276 individuals to swim to shore. Luckily, by the grace of God, everyone made it safely to shore. If a shipwreck wasn't traumatic enough, look at what happens to Paul next:

> Once we were safe on shore, we learned that we were on the island of Malta. The people of the island were very kind to us. It was cold and rainy, so they built a fire on the shore to welcome us. As Paul gathered an armful of sticks and was laying them on the fire, a poisonous snake, driven out by the heat, bit him on the hand. The people of the island saw it hanging from his hand and said to each other, "A murderer, no doubt! Though he escaped the sea, justice will not permit him to live." But Paul shook off the snake into the fire and was unharmed. The people waited for him to swell up or suddenly drop dead. But when they had waited a long time and saw that he wasn't harmed, they changed their minds and decided he was a god. (Acts 28:1–6)

The dude can't catch a break. First, he's imprisoned for no valid reason. Then he's beaten to inches of death. To spare his life, he suggests appealing to Caesar. On his way to this appeal, the boat that he's on gets annihilated by a storm. Now while he's stranded on an island, he gets bit by a snake. Not just any kind of garden snake but a deadly, poisonous snake. Have you heard of the phrase "When it rains, it pours?" This is like a torrential downpour in Paul's life.

The natives make a fire to warm the people, and it's that very fire that drew the snakes out. When you're passionate about anything in your life, that passion ignites a fire within your soul. It's that fire that propels you forward even in the face of adversity. Fire is a great thing, except when there's a fire ignited in your life, poisonous snakes will inevitably be drawn out. Paul has a fiery passion to spread the good news about Jesus. His life had purpose. That fire invited opposition. The poisonous snake bit Paul, but he didn't even give the snake the time of day. It's as if he swatted it away like a little fly. We know this because Luke wrote Acts. Luke was a doctor and left no details out of his writing. If you don't believe me, read through the book of Luke. It's the longest of the four Gospels. Paul was bit by a poisonous snake and simply shook it off back into the fire that it was drawn out by. Paul was way more focused on the mission at hand than the snakes that tried to kill him. With our eyes fixed on Jesus rather than the things that try to attack us, we too can fling the snakes that bite us off back into the fire our passion produces. With every type of opposition Paul faced, he was given a new opportunity to further his mission. Whenever he was in jail, he preached to people about Jesus. Now that he was stranded on an island, the same priority held true. After the whole snake incident, Paul was brought to the house of the chief official of the island. While at the house, Paul realized that the chief official's father was sick. Paul laid his hands on him, and God healed him. After this happened, the Bible says that ALL the sick people on the island came and were healed. If the shipwreck would have never happened, Paul would have never met all these people. Had Paul never met these people, who knows how long it would have been before they all met God? Through Paul's willingness, commitment, and obedience to God's Word, even in spite of the storms, many were healed and introduced to the love of God through miraculous signs. Three months after the shipwreck, they finally voyaged to Rome.

We all have traditions and routines that are a part of our daily lives. Healthy lives are built on healthy routines and good habits. Think of some routines that you have as a part of your life. For some, it's making a cup of tea before they go to bed. For others, it can be as simple as having coffee every morning before their day starts or going to the gym after lunch or ordering tacos every Tuesday from the same restaurant. Karen and I have routines with our dogs, Dallas and Peanut. For example, every night, we walk them before we wind down and get ready for bed. As soon as we come through the door after our walk, Peanut knows it is time to fight. Peanut is a tiny chi-weenie that thinks she's way tougher and bigger than she actually is. We walk through the door, and immediately, Peanut bolts over to the couch, to the same spot, and starts to bark at me. This bark is inviting me to come over to her so she can go crazy and bite my hand. There's something about my hand, my right hand to be specific, that she likes to unleash rage on. We've tried with Karen, but Peanut is more drawn to the white meat, I guess. After she's done tearing up my hand, it's treat time. Every night without fail. This is our daily tradition. I've developed some routines and traditions in my personal life as well. One of my favorite rituals to partake in is engaging the after-Sunday service relaxation mode. When you serve at church all Sunday morning, it can be pretty tiring. It's amazing, don't get me wrong. But for someone who is an introvert by nature, preaching and praying and talking all morning into the afternoon can be a bit draining. There's nothing more satisfying than giving your all on a Sunday morning, getting home, finding the perfect spot in your living room or on your bed, kicking off your socks, and slipping into your favorite slippers. The slippers are KEY. Gosh, my body is put at ease just thinking about my slippers. No matter how stressful the day is, no matter how tired I am, no matter what challenges come up, I know that there will be a moment that I'm at home in my slippers. There have been times, if I'm being completely honest, that something stressful will come up during the morning, and all I can think about is that moment that I know I'll be putting my slippers on. It WILL come. The thought of my slippers released peace and endurance to my heart.

Having vision for your life is an extremely useful tool when it comes to navigating through life's challenges. No matter how dark the storm may be, no matter how booming the thunder is, no matter how violent the gusts of wind are, you will make it through it. Why? Because God has a plan for your life. Sure, life might look different on the other side of the storm, but that's okay. If our lives looked the same from the moment we were born until the moment that we die, that's not truly living. Storms can be intimidating, but just know there's a God who loves you, is for you, is with you, and promises that He will turn it for your good. You will make it through this. The sun WILL shine again. When you believe that God's not done with you, it ignites a drive and passion to take on life's storms with boldness, confidence, and courage. You can make it through the storm. You got this.

FIRE

When you go through deep waters, I will be
with you. When you go through rivers of difficulty, you will not drown. When you walk
THROUGH THE FIRE OF OPRESSION,
you will not be burned up; the flames will not
consume you. (Isaiah 43:2, emphasis added)

The first part of this book was dedicated to going through the storm.
Storms look different for everyone, but we all go through them. This
next section of the book is going to dissect what going through the
fire looks like. Though fires are extremely different than storms, they
are still challenging to go through nonetheless. Maybe you're in the
fire right now and aren't even aware of it. I hope this section encourages you, challenges you, and helps you step in and through the fire.

7

WELCOME TO BABYLON

Do you like to travel? I actually love traveling. Let me clarify. I love being new places, but the act of traveling is exceedingly irritating. Remember? Can't they just invent teleporting already? Fun fact: there's actually a story in the book of Acts of God teleporting someone. Freakin' cool. Acts 8. Philip. Check it out. Lord, may that happen for me every time I need to travel. Being married to someone from a different culture (literally living most of her life in another country) is such an incredible experience. It truly opens your eyes to a different way of living than you're used to. I never knew that black beans with eggs for breakfast was a thing. Like I mentioned earlier in the book, Karen is Guatemalan. Not like Guatemalan roots but "grew up in Los Angeles" Guatemalan. Karen was born and raised in Guatemala. How did we meet, you ask? It's a funny story, really. I won't go into too much of the details, but it's one of those stories where you really have to stop and acknowledge how evidently God was in it. In December of 2015, Karen was visiting Los Angeles for the first time. One of her best friends lives here, so for her Christmas vacation from work, she decided to go on a little adventure. Karen had only been in America one other time when she visited her other friend in Florida the year prior. When Karen came to explore LA, little did she know that her friends were going to, without any prior planning, devise a plan to set her up with their gringo friend, Brandon. Unbeknownst to Karen's friend, her husband threw the idea out randomly one night. They busted out a picture of this white Californian youth pastor and asked Karen if she'd be up for a blind date. Simultaneous with this conversation, on my end, I receive the world's most random text from my friend Ivan, who I haven't talked with or spent time with for over three years. Mind you, this is 2015, and I just started youth pastoring at my church. I was a single youth pastor, which meant everyone and their grandma (literally) had a life mission to set me up with someone they knew. Thank God nothing ever worked. So I receive that text from Ivan that simply said, "Brandon! It's been a while, man. Hope all is well! Question: are you single?" Taking me a bit by surprise, I replied, "Hey, Ivan! Uh, yeah, I'm single. Why?" I could sense the amount of enthusiasm and excitement that Ivan had in his text messages. He proceeds to ask me if I'd be interested in going on a blind date with one of his and Irene's friends. I was about to reply with a kind yet solid no, because let's be honest, blind dates can be extremely awkward. Do they like me? Do I like them? Nobody got time for that. Before I could get the response text out, Ivan sent me a picture of Karen. I was stopped in my tracks. I swiftly deleted my original response and changed it to "I am in." Karen is SO beautiful. I would face even the most uncomfortable of scenarios if it meant getting to know THAT girl. So Ivan and Irene set up the double date and detailed out the place and time. In the communicational aspect of the developing of this potential relationship, they left out one tiny detail: Karen didn't live in the same country. Now, once I found out, it didn't scare me away like I think they anticipated. A majority of my good friends were either living in different states or countries. Long distance didn't intimidate me. We had a week to get to know each other, and in that week, we both knew that this was *the* person. God orchestrated the timing and details out beautifully. I could spend the rest of this book talking about how perfect and beautiful this week was, but I'll save that for another time. Long story short, in seven days, Karen and I were both convinced that God had brought us together. I'm not sure what you believe about this sort of stuff, but humor me for a second and look at the details of this particular story. Karen and I were both twenty-five, working at our churches, serving in the youth ministries, and are only TWO DAYS apart in age. One could argue that this is all coincidence, but I choose to look at it as God caring about the details of our lives and paving a perfect pathway for us to walk on. Where's the fun in thinking this is coincidence? Karen and I started dating long distance shortly after that, and within only a week of Karen going back to Guatemala, we had already planned a date for me to travel to Guatemala and meet her family. Some say we are crazy, and to that, I'd probably have to agree with you. We ARE crazy. But hey, here we are, happily married for three years now. Our craziness works. With a date to travel to Guatemala set, it hit me that I was about to travel to a country that I had never been to, nor have I ever traveled internationally alone. Whelp, here we go!

Guatemala is truly such a beautiful country. I might be a bit biased. When you fly in to Guatemala, if you happen to fly in the daytime, the first thing that catches your eye from outside the plane's window is a landscape of massive volcanoes enveloped in clouds. It's surreal. Not to mention Karen is from Guatemala. Any place that produces that type of person has to be fantastic. Within minutes after exiting our plane into the airport, I quickly realized I'm not in LA anymore. The language was different, the colors were different, and even the bathrooms were different. Okay, I need to get something off of my chest. It took me a good solid three days before I got the hang of not flushing toilet paper down the toilet after going to the bathroom. I understand that the plumbing isn't as powerful or efficient and that's why it can't be flushed, but from a gringo that never thought twice about toilet paper after the wipe, I needed a little grace. On my first trip to Guatemala, I can't even tell you how many people I met. I'm pretty sure Karen introduced me to the entire country. If my skin tone didn't give away the fact that I wasn't from there, when someone was introduced to me, it was a clear giveaway. I'm a hugger. Unashamedly so. I love hugs. Not in a weird, "I'm going to wait here awkwardly until you make eye contact with me and hug me kind of way" but in a bro-bro kind of way. Now, in the midst of a global pandemic, I'm not able to fulfill this desire as I used to, but the desire to give you a solid Christian side hug is still there. In Guatemala, if you're a guy being introduced to or greeting a girl, the customary thing to do is give a kiss on the cheek. This tripped me out at first, but it eventually grew on me in an endearing kind of way. The thing that was the most difficult habit for me to break out of was wanting to give Karen's guy friends a bro hug. Usually, if I say hi to a guy that I'm familiar with or to a good friend of a friend, my instinct is to give them a hug. In Guatemala, this seemed to take ALL the guys I was introduced to by surprise. Okay. The gringo gives hugs. The more awkward interactions I had, the more obvious it was that I was not from Guatemala. I was clearly away from home.

In this next part of the book, we will be looking into the lives of four individuals that spent a good amount of time in a place that was clearly not their home. Daniel, Hananiah, Mishael, and Azariah (commonly known as Daniel, Shadrach, Meshach, and Abednego) were four Israelites that were alive in the time of the Babylonian exile. An exile, just in case you're not familiar with what that is, is defined as the state of being barred from or expelled from one's native country. The Israelites were unfaithful to God. Therefore, God gave the Babylonians full reign to attack and conquer them. The Babylonians swooped in and began to flip everything upside down for the people of God. They took over and wanted to control everything—what they ate, how they dressed, what their names were, and even how they expressed their worship. There's a story in the book of Daniel that talks about how Shadrach, Meshach, and Abednego refused to give in to the Babylonian ways and, as a result of that, were thrown into a blazing furnace and left to die. They were subjected to going through the fire.

The fire is different than the storm. Unlike the storm, not everyone goes through the fire. Everyone will eventually go through a storm at some point in their lives, but fires, on the other hand, are reserved only for people who choose to go through them. Notice the word *oppression* in the scripture out of Isaiah 43:2 when referring to going through fire. It says, "When you walk through the fire of oppression, you will not be burned up. The flames will not consume you." The word *oppression* means prolonged cruel or unjust treatment or control. Specifically, in this chapter, I want to talk about what a life looks like when it's truly committed to and sold out to following Jesus. If you're reading this and you have given your life to Jesus already, this will help encourage you through the challenges associated with that decision. If you haven't given your life to Jesus yet, this portion of the book will inform you about what a life dedicated to Jesus is truly all about. I hope that after reading through the first portion of the book, you've decided to open your heart up to God. There's something about storms that help us realize our need for God. Storms show us how out of control we really are. Faith in Jesus comes with giving up control of our lives and trusting it to the care of God. Storms show us how small we really are. A relationship with God helps us to personally know the One who is bigger than the entire universe. Though life's situations are oftentimes out of our hands, Jesus's hands were pierced in order to open up the reality of Him walking through them with us. Life truly is fragile and brief. Having genuine hope, which comes only from Jesus, anchors us through storms that clock in at any level of intensity. Realizing that the storms we walk through in life aren't caused by God but rather are a result of the fallen world we live in can alleviate any amount of anger directed toward God and any doubt of His love for us. The fire of oppression is reserved for those who, by faith, accept Jesus into their hearts and walk out their new life. Keep in mind that fire is for Christians who genuinely walk out their faith. Saying you're a Christian and going to church doesn't make you a Christian any more than standing in a garage and saying you're a car makes you a car. Not wanting to come across as mean (no condemnation), but genuine Christians have a slight burnt smell whenever you come across them. Everyone has been called to take up a life that goes through the fire, but not everyone answers that call. The fire is a challenge, yes, but the fire is also an honor. The fire is excruciating and extremely difficult at times, but there's no place I'd rather be. The fire is a part of the lives of all who call upon the name of Jesus.

King Nebuchadnezzar was the king of Babylon at the time of this story taking place. We will call him Neb for short. Neb was absolutely bent on feeling power and of wielding a sense of control over the people. Babylon would change your name, attacking your identity. Babylon would force you to eat the way they did, defiling your personal convictions in regards to eating. Babylon would force you into worshiping their gods, causing you to give up your commitment to God. Neb wanted to tell you what was right, what was true, and what was important to you. He wanted to be your god. He wanted to be your everything. Neb loved the spotlight so much that he even had a golden statue of himself constructed. At a certain time of the day every day, music would play, and the people would be forced into bowing down and worshiping the statue. Talk about a golden ego. See what I did there?

This spirit that Babylon carried, this controlling spirit, is the same spirit that Christians combat even in today's society. Babylon tries to distort your identity, define what is true, and decide what you will worship. When you give your life to Jesus, a transformation takes place. Genuine relationship with Jesus changes everything about you inside and out. Of course, no one is perfect, even with Jesus, but once He is in your life, we begin a lifelong process of becoming more and more like Him. Referring to a new life in Him, the Bible says in 2 Corinthians 5:17, "Therefore, if anyone is in Christ, he is a new creation. The old has passed away; behold, the new has come." God doesn't just polish up the old parts of your life and make them shine. God creates something brand-new. If you polish a turd, it's still a turd. Just saying. God takes us and makes us into something new. When you were a little kid, do you remember playing with the toy that had you put the wooden pieces through holes that matched the shapes in another piece of wood? Even if you didn't own one personally, you know what I'm talking about. If you had a circle piece, you would put it in the circle hole. If you had a triangle piece, you put it in the triangle-shaped hole. So on and so forth. When you invite Jesus into your heart, for real, it's like He transforms you from being a circle piece to a triangle piece. You are a completely new shape. Of course, you can try to force into the mold of your old life, but it just won't fit the same. At least that's what it was like for me when I came to know Jesus personally. Prior to following Jesus, I had rough edges. Of course, I still have a few, but I'm saying MANY rough edges. I would cuss every other word, be consumed with my self-image, and so many other things that manifested as a result of my brokenness.

Cussing was a huge problem for me. I had a lot of anger buildup in my heart growing up, and that was an easy way of expressing it and letting it out. Just to give you an idea as to how bad the cussing was, in the sixth grade, my friend and I had a contest to see who could go the longest without saying a bad word. The prize was a Snickers bar. I'd do anything for a Snickers bar. I couldn't go more than three minutes without cussing. I remember the moment I started taking Jesus seriously like it was yesterday. I kid you not, I was cussing all the way up until this particular meeting, and after I encountered the reality of Jesus and responded, I walked out of that room with no desire at ALL to cuss. It didn't even hit me until like a month later when I had realized I haven't said any bad words. My entire vocabulary changed in an instance. Well, actually, what really happened was that my heart was transformed in that single moment. The Bible teaches us that out of the abundance of the heart, your mouth speaks. God changed my heart in that room. Sure, the situations that I walked through that caused a lot of brokenness in my heart were still present, but everything about how I approached them was different. My heart was different. The Bible also says that God can take our hearts of stone and give us hearts of flesh that feel things and are alive. The world will beat the feeling out of your heart until it's calloused over. You might be reading this right now with a hardened heart. Maybe it has been a while since you've allowed yourself to feel anything. My friend, that's not how God designed you to be. You're supposed to feel things. Your heart is designed to fill up with experiences and emotions, but because of the brokenness of this world we live in, our hearts can easily harden. With God though, we become new creations with new hearts that begin to feel again.

Not only does God transform our hearts, but He gives us an entirely new identity when we come to Him. The Bible says that we are literally adopted into His family when we believe. What an incredible thought to hold on to! When you're adopted into the family of God, you not only get access to everything that is His. You now carry His name. I don't know what kind of names you've picked up along the way in your lifetime, but God's name and identity for you wipes away all the negative names and leaves you only with truth that uplifts and encourages. Maybe you've picked up the name failure. God's name for you is victorious. Maybe you've picked up the name accident or mistake. God's name for you is planned with a purpose. Or maybe you have the name ugly or waste of space. God's name for you is masterpiece. I don't know who needs to read this, but I feel led to tell you that you are truly God's masterpiece. You are a work of art, His PRIZED possession. The enemy wants you to believe you are a broken mess. I want to remind you right now that God makes broken lives beautiful, and every mess becomes a message through God's grace. There are multiple times when God changes someone's name in the Bible—Abram to Abraham, Simon to Peter, Saul to Paul. There's something significant that takes place when you truly embrace the name that God gives you. You identify with what your name is. Have you ever looked up the meaning of your name? I think that's a pretty cool thing to do! While I've heard of people's names meaning warrior or conqueror, my name means grassy null. Brandon is a green hill. Epic, right? The spirit of Babylon will try to take the name that God has given you, change it, and disregard it. Daniel's name was changed to Belteshazzar, Hananiah's name was changed to Shadrach, Mishael was changed to Meshach, and Azariah was changed to Abednego. Babylon wants to change your name because when your name changes, your identity changes. When your identity changes, the way we act and react changes. Who you truly believe yourself to be and whose you are will be the driving force behind your life. If the world can change your name, it will cause you to question your identity. If the world can cause you to question your identity, it can successfully rob you of your ability to stand out and make a difference. We are supposed to stand out. That's exactly what the enemy wants. How has your environment tried to change your name?

In addition to Babylon wanting to change your identity, Babylon wants to tell you what truth is. Truth, in our day and age, is a tricky subject to address with others. On one hand, people avoid speaking truth because they are afraid it will hurt feelings. On the other hand, people define their own truth as whatever makes sense to them and leads to happiness. That definition of truth can be a very dangerous thing. What do you define as truth? For a lot of the youth that I do life with, their source of truth comes from what TikTok or YouTube influencers have to say. If you have over one hundred thousand followers, youth are more open to hearing your version of truth. This way of gathering truth is so dangerous. Where is the line drawn? Who determines what is true and what isn't? Your truth could contradict another person's version of truth. If we base our definition of what is true on how it makes us feel, we are in danger of defining truth for ourselves and stepping into God's intended place in our lives. Truth doesn't always feel good, but it will always set you free. For me, I believe that the Word of God is truth. Everything in it is truth. Hear me out. I'm sure that there are a lot of people reading this that don't agree with everything the Bible says. Let's just address the elephant in the room. A ton of people instantly disregard the Bible as truth whenever the topic of homosexuality comes up. I can't even tell you how many times I've been shut out of conversations the moment someone finds out that I'm a pastor. Let me be upfront and extremely honest right now. If you are reading this and are a part of the LGBTQ + community, I love you. God loves you. I'm sorry if you've ever been treated differently because of your preferences or lifestyle choices. When your heart breaks as a result of discrimination, God's heart breaks. You are His creation, and He cares about you. I may not necessarily agree with you, but that doesn't mean I don't love you. You probably don't agree with me on everything too. We don't have to agree on everything in order to treat each other with dignity, kindness, and love. If I'm being completely honest, whenever I get the opportunity to talk with someone new for the first time, I'll hold off telling them I'm a pastor for as long as I can. The moment they find out I'm a pastor, the dynamic of our conversation changes drastically. There's no such thing as a casual conversation anymore. People are either extremely interested in what I do (usually these are the Christians) or lose interest in talking to me (these are usually people who have lost interest in God), or their new life purpose is to trip me up and cause me to stumble in my faith (these are usually people who have been hurt by someone who calls themselves a Christian). On a flight back to LA from New York, Karen and I had the opportunity to have a very…we'll call it flavorful conversation with the guy who was sitting next to me. Before the plane took off, I opened up dialogue with him. By the way, I'm the type of person that will strike up a conversation with you on a plane. There's the type of people that put their hood on and try to zone out into their own world, and then there's people like me that try to talk to you. Sorry if you've ever been forced to sit next to a talker like me on a plane. Anyways, before the plane took off, we started talking. Five minutes in to our conversation, our new plane friend busted out a tiny vile of alcohol from his bag and offered me and Karen some. We kindly declined and continued to carry on our conversation. While still on the surface level of our talk, he asked me and Karen what we did. Trying to avoid it at all cost, he finally discovered we were pastors. As soon as this came into the open, I kid you not, his entire demeanor shifted. He was immediately on the defensive. When he heard that we are pastors, his response was simply "Interesting." I knew we were about to embark on an extremely long flight. Rather than wanting to have a conversation with us about our beliefs, he spent hours just trying to disprove Christianity and make us look stupid. Luckily, Karen's a graceful boss, and both of us together were able to keep it civil between us and our new conversing friend. It turns out that our New York friend grew up in the church and was extremely hurt by a pastor who exiled his friend from the school they were a part of when it came out that his best friend was gay. This was the first of many horribly hurtful experiences this man experienced in his lifetime from a Christian that slowly created a wedge between him and God. He was so hurt by people that called themselves Christians that he wanted nothing to do with the God that those individuals so-called worshiped. Because of our personal life experiences, we can reject things that are true simply because we don't agree with them. Like I mentioned earlier, I believe that the Bible is truth. The things written in it are straight from God's heart.

> All Scripture is inspired by God and is useful to
> teach us what is true and to make us realize what
> is wrong in our lives. It corrects us when we are

wrong and teaches us to do what is right. God
uses it to prepare and equip His people to do
every good work. (2 Timothy 3:16–17)

When approaching the Bible for truth, it's important to remember to mold your life around the Word, not the Word around your life. The moment we start molding the Word around our lives is the moment we begin defining our own truth. It's also important to note that following God and searching for truth isn't just gathering a list of rules to follow. The more you read the Bible in its entirety, you begin to learn God's character. God is love. If you forget that, look no further than reading through the account of Jesus's life in the Gospels. The individuals that Jesus got into arguments the most with were the Pharisees, the ones who followed the law, a list of rules, to a T. The Bible says that Jesus is full of grace and truth. Truth without grace is legalism, and it pushes people away from God with an unreachable, unattainable standard. Grace without truth is shallow and meaningless. Note how grace comes before truth though. Jesus always leads with grace. He doesn't dismiss the truth and the standards that are in place to ensure a whole and satisfying life, but He cares more about showing the individual how much He loves them before telling them what they've done is wrong. I've noticed, at least in my own personal life, the more I love Jesus and the more I'm consumed with my relationship with Him, the less I think about following rules, and the more my life aligns with following His standards. Be someone who has a heart to learn. Be someone who is teachable and moldable. Let God begin shaping your understanding of truth, and I promise it will set you free. Ask yourself this question: "How do I determine what is truth in my life?" In a society that flaunts so many different versions of the truth, your answer to that question is extremely, EXTREMELY important.

Lastly, Babylon wants to tell you what to worship. Worship isn't just a term that's limited to Christianity. Worship, simply put, is to revere, honor, treasure, look up to, bow down before, and be devoted to. As a Christian, the ultimate goal is to devote all of our worship to God. When you truly realize how much He has done for you, how much He has sacrificed for you, how crazy about you He is, and how good He is, the only logical response is to live a life of worship unto Him. What you worship in your life is what is most important to you. It's where your dedication is assigned to. What you worship is a result of what is top priority to you. Whether you're aware of it or not, you are always worshiping something. You could worship your job, your clothes, your car, or your relationships. Really, anything that you can invest time and focus into can be a recipient of your worship. Here's the thing, though. Humans, I believe, were created to worship God and God alone. It's written into our DNA. This is why it's such a beautiful thing when it clicks in someone's heart and their worship is directed in the right way. This is also why the enemy wants to steal and own your worship. Satan wants to be your focus, because when he is your focus, your focus isn't on God. THAT'S what he wants. In the book of Daniel, Babylon changed Daniel and his friend's names and challenged them in what to eat. It wasn't until Shadrach, Meshach, and Abednego refused to worship the golden statue of Neb that they were forced into the fire.

Because they refused to bow down to Neb and give him their worship, Shadrach, Meshach, and Abednego were thrown into a fiery furnace to be killed. From now on, I'll refer to Shadrach, Meshach, and Abednego as the three. Let's just say that writing their names out every other sentence cramps the fingers a tad bit. To allow complete insight into what this story tells us, let's read it straight from the Bible:

> When you hear the sound of the horn, flue, zither, lyre, harp, pipes, and other musical instruments, bow to the ground to worship King Nebuchadnezzar's gold statue. Anyone who refuses to obey will immediately be thrown into a blazing furnace. So, at the sound of the musical instruments, all the people, whatever their race or nation or language, bowed to the ground and worshiped the gold statue that King Nebuchadnezzar had set up. But some of the

astrologers went to the king and informed on the Jews. They said to King Nebuchadnezzar, "Long live the king! You issued a decree requiring all the people to bow down and worship the gold statue when they hear the sound of the horn, flute, zither, lyre, harp, pipes, and other musical instruments. That decree also states that those who refuse to obey must be thrown into a blazing furnace. But there are some Jews—Shadrach, Meshach, and Abednego, whom you have put in charge of the province of Babylon. They pay no attention to you, Your Majesty. They refuse to serve your gods and do not worship the gold statue you have set up." Then Nebuchadnezzar flew into a rage and ordered that Shadrach, Meshach, and Abednego be brought before him. When they were brought in, Nebuchadnezzar said to them, "Is it true, Shadrach, Meshach, and Abednego, that you refuse to serve my gods or to worship the gold statue I have set up? I will give you one more chance to bow down and worship the statue I have made when you hear the sound of the musical instruments. But if you refuse, you will be thrown immediately into the blazing furnace. And then what god will be able to rescue you from my power?" Shadrach, Meshach, and Abednego replied, "O Nebuchadnezzar, we do not need to defend ourselves before you. If we are thrown into the blazing furnace, the God whom we serve is able to save us. He will rescue us from your power, Your Majesty. But even if He doesn't, we want to make it clear to you, Your Majesty, that we will never serve your gods or worship the gold statue you have set up." Nebuchadnezzar was so furious with Shadrach, Meshach, and Abednego that his face became distorted with rage. He commanded that the furnace be heated seven times hotter than usual. Then he ordered some of the strongest men of his army to bind Shadrach, Meshach, and Abednego and throw them into the blazing furnace. So, they tied them up and threw them into the furnace, fully dressed in their pants, turbans, robes, and other garments. And because the king, in his anger, had demanded such a hot fire in the furnace, the flames killed the soldiers as they threw the three men in. So, Shadrach, Meshach, and Abednego, securely tied, fell into the roaring flames. But suddenly, Nebuchadnezzar jumped up in amazement and exclaimed to his advisors, "Didn't we tie up three men and throw them into the furnace?" "Yes, Your Majesty, we certainly did," they replied. "Look!" Nebuchadnezzar shouted. "I see four men, unbound, walking around in the fire unharmed! And the fourth looks like a god!" Then Nebuchadnezzar came as close as he could to the door of the flaming furnace and shouted: "Shadrach, Meshach, and Abednego, servants of the Most High God, come out! Come here!" So, Shadrach, Meshach, and Abednego stepped out of the fire. Then the high officers, officials, governors, and advisers crowded around them and saw that the fire had not touched them. Not a hair on their heads was singed, and their clothing was not scorched. They didn't even smell of smoke! (Daniel 3:5–27)

Wow! Just sit and take that in for a moment. The three refused to give in to the pressure that Babylon was placing on them to conform. Because they never gave in, they were thrown into a literal fire. The same spirit that fueled Babylon's desire for control and worship still rages in our world today. My question to you, before moving any further, is this: are you willing to go through the fire? If you're feeling pressure right now from the world around you, you're in the right place. When you don't eat what they want you to eat, when you don't worship the things that are right in front of you, when you hold on to the identity that God has given you, you are subjected to pressure and in danger of the fire. In the next two chapters of this section, we will continue to look at this concept of going through the fire and see how we can apply it to our lives. Get ready to get burned.

8

THE FIRE IS NECESSARY

I love fire. Not in a pyromaniac kind of obsessive way, but I really do love it. There's nothing more relaxing to me than sitting by a bon-fire at night on the beach with a beat-up acoustic guitar, stars in the clear sky, and some gooey, sticky s'mores. Fire warms you when you're cold, lights up dark rooms with mood-lit candles, and let's not forget the most important use for fire of all time—fireworks. You can't spell firework without fire. There's something inside my soul that ignites when I get to play with fireworks. Did I say play with? I meant to say ignite with the proper safety measures in place. I've loved fireworks for as long as I can remember. When I was but a wee little lad, my parents would let me hold sparklers on the Fourth of July and throw those little white poppers on the ground. I would grasp the sparkler in my hands as hard as I could, eagerly waiting for the match to come in contact with the tip of it and ignite it. The bright red, white, and blue sparkles would light up the night. I even would take the sparkler and write my name in the blacktop right in front of my par-ents' house. The poppers were fun too. While others were running around throwing them at each other, I was content with keeping to myself and throwing them down at my feet. The loud pop and tiny spark filled me with so much joy and excitement. As I grew older, I became a bit more…let's say creative in how I experimented with fireworks. Me and my neighborhood friends, Tyler and Chico, would have weekly fire nights. We will call him Chico to protect any innocent bystanders. Fire night was the night of the week that I looked forward to the most. Every week, the day that fire night happened would vary, but it was tradition. It was going to happen. The first rule of fire night was that it was going to happen. The second rule of fire night was to not speak of fire night. Before you start jumping to conclusions and start casting your judgments, let me put your concerns at ease and say that nothing was ever damaged (beyond repair) and no one was hurt (severely). We would come together at a disclosed location and just play with fire. There were some nights when we would just sit and burn random things like paper, pencils, shoelaces, and other little things, you know. Other nights, we would get creative with hair spray or other flammable liquids. We would write our names out on the sidewalk with the hair spray, light it with a match, and watch our names light up. Okay, in hindsight, this might not have been the wisest use of my time, but it shaped me into who I am today! Fire nights have formed me. We would normally stick to little tasks, burning tiny objects or hair spray, but there is one night in particular I will never forget. Tyler and I went over to Chico's house like we always did, except this time, there was a sparkle in Chico's eyes unlike anything I've ever seen before. He told us that his cousin picked up fireworks for him on his way home from the beach. Chico was PUMPED to use these fireworks. These fireworks weren't the ones that make pretty fountains of color or whistled around on the ground. These were the kind that simply went boom. They were tiny black fireworks that were called black panthers. Terrifying, I know. We lit some and threw them around, and they did just what we expected them to do, go boom. This week's fire night was a success. The next morning, I get a call from Chico. Chico apparently found two more black panthers that we didn't get to light the night before. Of course, this couldn't wait until next week. Chico and I met at our community pool to see how we can put those black panthers to good use. We wandered around for a few minutes until I was struck with a genius idea. We would go into the bathroom, flip the little metal warming cup on the bottom of the hand dryer upside down, put the black panther in it, and make a long fuse out of toilet paper. We would light the toilet paper fuse on fire and then run outside the bathroom until it exploded. Foolproof. So we did just that. We executed the plan with no flaw. Flipped the little hand warmer upside down, put the black panther in it, created a long fuse out of toilet paper, ran it on the ground, prepared to light it on fire, lit it on fire, and watched it run down the toilet paper on the ground into the hand warmer. We ran outside of the bathroom and waited for our grand finale. Everything seemed to work fine, until it didn't. As we waited outside the bathroom for our big boom, we heard nothing but silence. Deafening silence. You could cut the tension with a butter knife. When we lit the fuse before we ran outside, and we saw it go up into the hand warmer. We swear we did. One minute turned to two. Two minutes turned to three. We couldn't take the waiting any longer. I busted into the bathroom and peeked my head over into the hand warmer where the black panther was, and suddenly without warning, let's just say our plan worked. It just needed a little gust of air to finish the process. The black panthers are loud in an open space. Imagine for a second, if you would, how loud the black panther was in a small one-person bathroom that was layered with tile. This was a whole new type of loud. My ears were ringing for like twenty minutes after that. I thought I was, for sure, going deaf. Praise report: I didn't go deaf, and now I have this epic story to share with you. Thank you, Chico.

The fire that was involved in fire nights was entertaining and fun. The fire that warms you in a fireplace on a cold winter night is comforting. The fire that melts the wax of a candle in your home is relaxing. What about the fire that we talked about in the last chapter? What about the fire of oppression that Isaiah 43 talks about? That fire is necessary. Necessary for what? I'm so glad you asked!

Like what we established in the previous chapter, going through the fire is entirely up to you. It's your choice. By putting your faith in Jesus, walking out that faith, and looking different than the world around you, the fire is an inevitability. Shadrach, Meshach, and Abednego refused to give in to the pressures that Babylon forcefully placed on to them, resulting in them being thrown into a fire. When we too resist the temptation to conform, the fire of oppression is looming. There's something beautiful that the fire produces in the lives of those who are brave enough to go through it. As followers of Jesus, it should be our goal to look more and more like Him every day of our lives. In order to achieve that, we must allow God to put us through the fire.

Throughout the entire Bible, there are many names that God is identified by. All of which reveal a different aspect of His character. For example, God in Psalm 23 is referred to as our shepherd. This name has such a deep implication to how we can relate with Him. A shepherd cares for, directs, and corrects their sheep. God is also referred to as a gardener in John 15. A gardener does everything in their ability to make sure their plants are healthy. If we allow God to be our gardener, we give Him free reign to cut the areas off in our lives that don't need to be there. In the Psalms, there are SO many names that God has: redeemer, light, salvation, refuge, strong tower, healer, hiding place, victory, and provider, just to name a few. One of the most interesting descriptive names that God is referred to, in my opinion, is found in the book of Malachi 3:3: "He will sit like a refiner of silver…"

Redeemer, healer, victor—those all are rather straightforward names. God as a silversmith, on the other hand, takes a little digging to understand. When you really stop and think about the implications of that statement, it opens up your heart to a whole new understanding of Who God is and how He takes care of us. Here's the thing with silversmiths—they use fire as a tool to accomplish their goals with their silver. God not only allows us to go through the fire, He uses the fire to bring out the best in us. In the various biblical references to refining precious metals, it's usually figurative to illustrate the kind of trials that God's children are called to go through. The refining of silver is a stressful, challenging, and time-consuming process, but the end product is absolutely breathtaking. Let's take a deeper look into what silversmiths do to catch just how amazing it is to have God as our silversmith.

When people work with fire to create art, it fascinates me. One thing in particular that blows me away is the art of glass blowing. It looks so magical when the artists hold the glass in the furnace on a blowing tube, pull it out, and start spinning it while blowing into it at the same time! How in the world does glass get so hot that it starts to melt? There's a show on Netflix that Karen and I binged quick-fast called *Blown Away*. It truly blew me away (can't stop with the puns). These artists would create different colors, textures, images, and sculptures, all from glass. In order to transform the raw materials into glass, they need to be placed into a furnace that reaches over 2,000 degrees Fahrenheit. Let that sink in for a second. Over two thousand degrees. I feel like I'm dying when it gets to 100 degrees in a Californian summer. There's something significant that takes place in the heat of a fire though, something that wouldn't have taken place without it getting hotter. When a silversmith places silver into the fire, they actually place the silver in the middle of the fire where the temperature is the highest. Have you ever felt that God has not only let you go through a fire, but that fire is cranked to the highest setting? I've definitely felt like that. At the time of Karen and me losing Asher, it honestly felt like it was one unfortunate thing after another happening. It's as if each month in 2019, the heat of our fire was being turned up another ten degrees. We knew (this isn't an exaggeration) around fifteen other couples that were pregnant at the same time we were. They all had their babies without any compli-cations, while Karen and I sat and watched other people beginning their families. With each new picture posted, with every pregnancy announcement, our fire was turned up another degree. It's like some-thing in the air was making people pregnant! It was literally CRAZY. Let me just say, for the record, that I'm genuinely so happy for our friends that had babies. We celebrate with you, are happy for you, and pray for continued health for you and your family. It just makes me sad to remember the time we had with Asher and the memories we will never get to share with him. On top of all the baby business, it's like everything else decided to hit the fan as well. Karen and I got sick more often than we usually ever do in 2019, our car was totaled, Karen got injured a couple of times, Dallas, our dog, had a really bad seizure and needed to start taking medicine, and on top of all that, I started to develop really bad anxiety, panic attacks, and depression. I don't say all of this to make you to feel bad for us. I say all of this to show you that when the fire's hot, it keeps getting hotter.

The purpose of putting silver into the hottest part of the fire, as a silversmith, is to burn away all the impurities. If you put a piece of silver into a microwave, expecting the same result, you'll be highly disappointed. God desires to see you pure, and that purity is made possible by the fire. Sin stains us. The more life we live, the more scratches, dings, and blemishes we acquire.

In my humble opinion, one of the greatest inventions of all time is the Tide pen. It is BRILLIANT. Literally every time I where a white shirt, I get a stain on it. It's like there's a food magnet woven into the fabric of my white shirts. Coffee, tea, mustard, ketchup, you name it. If I'm wearing a white shirt, it's not a matter of if I'll get it on there. It's when. If I get a stain on my shirt, it's over. I can't focus. I can't even concentrate until I'm able to go change. When you have a stain, doesn't it feel like that's the only thing people see when you run into them? I'm trying to make eye contact with you, and I see your eyes drifting down to my stain. I SEE YOU. Stains stress me out. With the Tide pen, whenever you get a stain, you bust that bad boy out and dab a little magic juice on it, and within minutes, that stain is obliterated. Have you ever seen those OxiClean commercials? The ones where they take a pair of pants that have a ton of grass and poop stains on them and put them into a bowl that has water with OxiClean in it? The bowl dissolves all the stains, and the pants are taken out looking brand-new. In life, whenever we obtain a stain, that stain remains until we decide to go through the fire. (That kind of rhymed.) When we sin, though the act only lasts for a moment, there is always residual stains left behind. Whether we participate in the sin ourselves or are a recipient of someone else's sin, there is always a stain. What kind of stains are you walking around with right now? Maybe you're struggling with an addiction right now with porn, drugs, alcohol. I remember the first time I was introduced to porn when I was in the fifth grade. It was like I was exposed to something that hooked its claws into my heart and brain. I couldn't get enough of it. I didn't feel good after looking at it, but each time an opportunity arose, I would find myself going back. It altered the way I viewed girls and the way I viewed myself. Each time stained me. The enemy wants to stain you as much as he can because each stain will remind you how you fell short. It's easy to only look at the stains, right? When I get a stain on my shirt, no matter how big it is, that's all I can see in the mirror. It wasn't until I met Jesus that the purification process in my heart and brain began. I stand here today not only completely free from porn addiction but purified from all the residual stains. I want to tell you that the same is possible for you.

Isaiah 1:18 says, "Though your sins are like scarlet, I will make them as white as snow. Though they are red like crimson, I will make them as white as wool." Sin stains, but God's love purifies. The primary tool that God uses in the purification process is fire. The next time you feel oppressed because of following Jesus, remember that God is letting you go through that fire to purify you. I've known people that have been kicked out of their homes because of following Jesus. I've also heard of people losing jobs, getting made fun of, losing friends, and getting yelled at all because of being Christian. Jesus says in Matthew 5:11–12, "How ecstatic you can be when people insult and persecute you and speak all kinds of cruel lies about you because of your love for me! So, leap for joy—since your heavenly reward is great. For you are being rejected the same way the prophets were before you." Let God place you in the hottest part of the fire. By doing this, you will see the stains of sin begin to burn up and dissolve one by one. Remember how when Shadrach, Meshach, and Abednego were thrown into the fire, not only were the ropes that were used to bind them burned, even the guards that held them captive burned up too! If you feel bound up or held captive by a certain addiction or sin, it's time to take a step into the fire. It's time to say yes to Jesus and start getting bold. If you say you follow Him but no one around you knows what you believe, are you really? I don't say this to condemn you but rather to challenge you! When you stand up for Christ, when you boldly follow Him, you can't help but look different. Jesus says this in the passage below right after He taught about the insults and persecutions:

Your lives light up the world. Let others see your light from a distance, for how can you hide a city that stands on a hilltop? And who would light a lamp and then hide it in an obscure place? Instead, it's placed where everyone in the house can benefit from its light. So don't hide your light! Let it shine brightly before others, so that the commendable things you do will shine as light upon them, and then they will give their praise to your Father in heaven. (Matthew 5:14–16)

Standing for Jesus gives you access to the fire, and the fire purifies your heart and mind.

When we realize that the fire is a necessary step in our purification process, it can eventually adjust our perspective of the fire. When our perspective of the fire changes, we will no longer be tempted to hold on to bitterness, which can come as a result of people's persecution toward us. Bitterness is a stain that eventually eats away at your heart. Bitterness is an emotional cancer, spreading all throughout your soul until it devours everything. We must remember that when people are hurting or insecure, the chances of them hurting those around them are extremely high. When our hearts are pure, rather than blaming those who hurt us, we are able to bless them. Hebrews 12:15 says, "Look after each other so that none of you fails to receive the grace of God. Watch out that no poisonous root of bitterness grows up to trouble you, corrupting many." When we learn to bless rather than to blame, our hearts are truly set free. This level of freedom is only attainable from going through the fire.

Persecution is something that the early church was well aware of and familiar with. Christians were hunted, placed on trial, mocked, murdered, chased, and more just because they followed Jesus. The book of 1 Peter was written to Christians who were scattered around as a result of harsh persecution. Christians were being murdered, and because of this eminent danger, the church was forced to spread. With this context in mind, Peter writes this:

> And through your faith, God is protecting you by His power until you receive this salvation, which is ready to be revealed on the last day for all to see. So be truly glad. There is wonderful joy ahead, even though you must endure many trials for a little while. These trials will show you that your faith is genuine. It is being tested as fire tests and purifies gold, though your faith is far more precious than mere gold. So, when your faith remains strong through MANY TRIALS, it will bring you much praise and glory and honor on the day when Jesus Christ is revealed to the whole world. (1 Peter 1:5–8)

The fire of persecution changes those who are brave enough to endure it. The fire isn't easy. The fire isn't comfortable. The fire burns. Sometimes, when you're in the fire, it's easy to forget that you're never alone. I'll never forget the season when I first started following Jesus. I was still in high school when I gave my life to Jesus. In school, none of my friends were Christians. Well, some said they were Christians, but none of them were really living out their faith. When I started to change as a result of my faith, they started to distance themselves from me. I stopped talking like they did, I stopped dressing like they did, and I stopped enjoying the things they enjoyed. Inevitably, distance between us started to grow. In the middle of the fire, in the moments when you might feel the most alone, never forget that Jesus is right there with you. When Shadrach, Meshach, and Abednego were thrown into the fire, King Neb was in shock at the realization that there were four people in the fire. He was convinced that he had thrown only three men into the fire, and when he was observing this miracle taking place, he counted four individuals. The Bible even quotes King Neb saying "It even looks like a Son of Man!" Jesus was literally IN THE FIRE WITH THEM. This is an incredible truth about how God walks with us. Not only does He let us go through the fire because He knows it's necessary for our development, He takes every step through the fire with us.

When I was sixteen, I got my first job working at the food area in Target. It's pretty comical how the whole job interview went down because I honestly wasn't trying to get the job at Target. I was trying to get a job at Hot Dog on a Stick, and I wanted that job more. I mean, come on. They got to wear gym shorts as part of their work uniform. I only went to Target because one of the cool kids in my English class was going to turn in an application and invited me to tag along. Of course, I went with him because I wanted him to like me. We went to Target, he started to fill out one of the electronic applications, and to help appease my boredom, I started to fill out an application too. As soon as I finished filling out the personal portion of the application, there was one final step that needed to be done in order to complete the whole thing. There was a red phone next to the computer, and I needed to simply pick up the phone and let them know that I was done filling out the application. Next thing I know, both me and my English buddy were being escorted to the upstairs offices to take part in an on-the-spot interview. I thought these things took time! Whenever I turned in an application prior to this moment, I always wore a button-up shirt and tie because I wanted to make a good first impression. In this particular interview, I had my holy jeans, my dirty black Hot Topic sweatshirt, and my nasty checkered Vans on. I was dressed appropriately for a rock concert, not a work interview. Both my English buddy and I interviewed at the same time. After thirty minutes worth of questions, I emerged from that office with a job offer and a day and time to come back for orientation. To make the situation more awkward, my English buddy didn't get a job offer. Whelp. Let me just tell you how uncomfortable that ride back to school was. I would have rather been anywhere else but there. It's all good though. I got a job.

Target was truly a great place to work. I learned a lot about responsibility, respect, and work ethic in my almost eight years of being there. In my tenure at Target, I had the opportunity to work under a wide variety of different management styles. Each manager had their own approach to leadership and leading teams of people. There were the managers that were overly invested, the managers that weren't invested at all, and the managers that I believe balanced the two extremely well. From the perspective of a greasy sixteen-year-old that was at his first job, let me tell you that when a manager actually worked with me and showed me how to do something rather than just sit on a high horse and make demands, I felt way more supported and inspired to get my job done. We must remember that God will not only never let us go through anything alone, He completely relates with the feelings of pressure and burning that we feel.

On the greatest rescue mission of all time, God literally put on flesh and bones, left His throne in heaven, and came to the world He created. Jesus, though He is one hundred percent God, is one hundred percent human. Jesus felt pain. Jesus experienced temptations. Jesus was rejected. Jesus was targeted. He felt then what we feel now. Maybe right now you feel down because some of your friends have distanced themselves from you. Think about how Jesus felt when one of His best friends sold Him out to be killed. Judas was one of the twelve closest individuals to Jesus during the time of His earthly ministry. Not only did Judas sell Jesus out. Peter, another one of Jesus's best friends, denied that he even knew who Jesus was. Rejection was an emotion that Jesus was very familiar with.

> If the world hates you, remember that it hated Me first. The world would love you as one of its own if you belonged to it, but you are no longer part of the world. I chose you to come out of the world, so it hates you. Do you remember what I told you? "A slave is not greater than the master." Since they persecuted Me, naturally they will persecute you. And if they had listened to Me, they would listen to you. They will do all this

to you because of Me, for they have rejected the
One who sent Me. (John 15:18–21)

When we go through the fire, we are exposed to experiences that
we wouldn't have been exposed to if we had never placed our faith
in Jesus. These experiences are a key factor in molding and shaping
us into the best version of ourselves. You guys know who Paul is at
this point in reading the book, but I want you to look at words that
came from Paul while he was locked up in prison for being a follower
of Christ:

> I was circumcised when I was eight days old. I
> am a pure-blooded citizen of Israel and a member
> of the tribe of Benjamin...a real Hebrew if there
> ever was one! I was a member of the Pharisees,
> who demand the strictest obedience to the Jewish
> law. I was so zealous that I harshly persecuted the
> church. And as for righteousness, I obeyed the
> law without fault. I once thought these things
> were valuable, but now I consider them as worth-
> less because of what Christ has done. Yes, every-
> thing else is worthless when compared with the
> infinite value of knowing Christ Jesus my Lord.
> For His sake I have discarded everything else,
> counting it all as garbage, so that I could gain
> Christ and become one with Him. I no longer
> count on my own righteousness through obeying
> the law; rather, I become righteous through faith
> in Christ. (Philippians 3:5–8)

Reading through that letter, you can sense the different things
that have burnt off of Paul as a result of numerous trips through the
fire. This is a natural part of the process for anyone who calls on the
name of the Lord! You can count on it happening.

The book of Jeremiah is written by the prophet Jeremiah, who was actually alive during the time of the Babylonian exile, the same period that we read about Daniel and his friends experiences. Jeremiah was a prophet who spoke on behalf of God to His people before and during their exile. Before the exile, Jeremiah warned the people to turn back to God and turn away from all their sinful ways. When they continued to reject his advice and counsel, that's what eventually led to God allowing Babylon to conquer Israel. During the exile, the time of great pressure and persecution (literally the fire), Jeremiah wrote these words from God to encourage those who were in the middle of the trial:

> Jeremiah wrote a letter from Jerusalem to the elders, priests, prophets, and all the people who had been exiled to Babylon by King Nebuchadnezzar… This is what the Lord of Heaven's Armies, the God of Israel, says to all the captives He has exiled to Babylon from Jerusalem: "Build homes, and plan to stay. Plant gardens, and eat the food they produce. Marry and have children. Then find spouses for them so that you may have many grandchildren. Multiply! Do not dwindle away! For I know the plans I have for you," says the Lord. "They are plans for good and not for disaster, to give you a future and a hope. In those days when you pray, I will listen. If you look for Me wholeheartedly, you will find Me." (Jeremiah 29:1, 4–6, 11–12)

God has plans for you in the fire. Plans that wouldn't have ever been available had there been no fire. Rather than allowing the flames discourage you and cause you to abandon the faith, embrace them, set up your home in them, and allow God's faithfulness to bring you through them.

Flames also have the ability to make you stronger. Shou sugi ban is an ancient Japanese technique that preserves wood by charring it with fire. This technique of burning the wood without allowing it to completely catch on fire results in a number of benefits. Wood that has been through this treatment is rot-resistant, pest-resistant, weather-resistant, ironically fire-resistant, and UV-resistant. The more times we walk through the fire as a result of our faith in Christ, the stronger we truly become.

The ultimate goal of any follower of Christ while here on earth should be to look more and more like Jesus each and every day. There's something about the process of going through fire that helps us to achieve that goal. When a silversmith places silver into the hottest part of the fire, the silversmith knows when the silver is done with the process when they can see their face in the reflection of the silver. The more you reflect God, the more the enemy can't stand you. Have you ever been in a relationship with someone that ended in a breakup? You begin to hate every little thing that reminds you of that person. The cars, the perfume, the food, the TV shows—literally everything that sparks even the slightest memory. When you follow Jesus for real, you begin to reflect Jesus, and the enemy hates that. The more that we boldly step into the fire, the more we will reflect our Father. The fire is necessary to purify, liberate, and cleanse us of the things that have so easily attached themselves onto us as a result of our journey through this life.

9

FIRE INSURANCE

Do you like sports? I like sports. I like watching sports way more than playing them. When it comes to playing sports, I am extremely average. In elementary school, whenever the opportunity arose for a game that entailed picking teams, I was never the first one picked. Come to think of it, I wasn't even the second, third, or sixth one picked. Usually, it came down to me and one or two others. If I wasn't picked last, I was VERY close to it. This explains why I now play the guitar. When I was younger, I attempted to play recreational sports. When I say attempted, I truly mean just that. While many of the other kids in my grade played tackle football, I played flag football. In hindsight, I'm actually really thankful that my parents didn't let me play tackle football no matter how badly I wanted to. I'm not sure if I'd be here still today if I had stepped into tackle football. I was and still am a fragile human being emotionally and physically. Instead of playing overhand throw baseball, my parents enrolled me in underhand softball. Still elements of competition, just way less demanding. Again, I was a fragile human being. I'll never forget the first time I tried out roller hockey. Note the roller instead of ice. Ice hockey was too fast-paced and violent. I hope this helps to give you insight into why I am the way I am. Right before the roller hockey season started, my parents took me to a local store called The Hockey Stop to purchase all my necessary gear. I got a helmet, pads, roller blades, and a left-handed stick. Keep in mind, I'm right-handed. For some reason, at this age in my life, I was determined to be left-handed. I still don't understand why. Anyways, I was geared up and ready for my career in roller hockey to begin. When the practices and workshops began, the only thing I had interest in while the other kids were learning drills was checking. Checking, in hockey, is when you hit someone into the walls to try and get them to lose momentum or to lose the puck. Only instead of checking other people into the walls, I was checking myself into the walls. This really happened. While the other kids were skating around, probably preparing to play some scrimmages, I was off doing my own thing, checking myself into the side walls. What I would give to see some footage of that today. As a child, I played roller hockey, flag football, and underhand slow-pitch softball. Needless to say, I was drawn, ever so profoundly, to music.

When I just got hired as a youth pastor for my church, I wanted to find any opportunity that I could to build relationship with the other guys there. I mean, I didn't know anyone at the church before I went there, so anything that I could do to get to know them better, I wanted to be a part of. It just so happened that the church had a softball team, and they invited me to be a part of it. Taking into consideration my epic resume of sports involvement, it was a no-brainer. When we started practicing, it was very clear to them and me why I was never picked first in my elementary years. Our first game was against a team called Balls Deep. This is real life, guys. Church Team versus Balls Deep. Yep. I remember it like yesterday. I was pumped up and ready to go crazy. My position, just in case you were wondering, was catcher. Though that sounds pretty epic, think about it: catcher in slow-pitch softball. My only job, practically, was to throw the ball back to the pitcher when the pitch was bad or the batter missed the ball. Let's be honest though. No one misses in slow-pitch, grown-man softball. Balls Deep was up first, and we held them to two runs. Three outs meant that Church Team is now up to bat. They put me fifth. I was ready. All four batters before me got on base with no struggle. This gave me a glimmer of hope. I was up next, so I started to do some warm-up swings outside the dugout. It was a brisk fall night. My heart started pounding in my chest. I was ready to make a statement with that bat. I stepped up to the plate and looked the older gentleman who was pitching square in the eyes, I tapped the plate with my bat and was ready. One, miss. Two, miss. Now before I tell you what happened next, I need you to remember that I play music, I pastor, and I'm fragile. Don't judge me. I took a deep breath, in through the nose and out the mouth. I was ready for my final pitch. I see the softball release from the pitcher's hand. I can tell it was going to hit the home plate, which was going to be a strike in slow-pitch softball. It was slow motion. I step forward with my left foot and swing with all my might. Nothing but air. I struck out in slow-pitch softball. It takes some serious skill to do that, if you ask me. We ended up scoring in that inning, putting us back on top. A couple of innings passed, and I was given the opportunity to heal from my bruised ego. Sure enough, it eventually came time for my next up at bat. Sweet redemption. When I picked up the bat to start warming up, there was a voice that started to whisper doubts to my mind. I was actually really afraid to go back out there and humiliate myself again. I also didn't want to let my team down. There was that too. As I stepped out to the plate, I saw the outfield shift forward. This was the fuel to the fire burning in my soul. I was determined to show them that this skinny white boy had some gusto. No matter how the first pitch was, I determined that I was going to (excuse my language) hit the poo-poo out of that softball. The pitch was up, and I saw it in slow motion. I took a deep breath, stepped forward, and hit that ball to the depths of the outfield. Friends, it was a beautiful moment. Seeing the ball fly over the outfielder's head was one of the highlights of my short-lived slow-pitch softball career. We went on to lose that game, but THAT'S NOT THE POINT, OKAY? I didn't let worry or fear dictate how I played the game or not. The great Babe Ruth said, "Don't let the fear of striking out stop you from playing the game." Fear is something that is so real, and fear is the driving factor in preventing many people from stepping into the fire. What if I told you that there were ways to overcome fear? What if I told you that fear no longer has any power over you? What if I told you that you no longer have to be a slave to fear? Fear drives the decisions of so many. Fear is at the root of a majority of the bad things that happen in this life. Think about it. Fear of failure could potentially drive someone to manipulate or cheat to come out on top. Fear of rejection could lead someone to act out of their character or compromise their standards. Working with youth, I've heard so many stories of students doing things they wouldn't normally ever do simply because they want to fit in and be accepted. The fear of loss can actually rob someone of enjoying present moments. Have you ever been somewhere and all you can think about are the what-ifs? I can't even tell you how much my mind is bombarded with the what-ifs. Worry has actually been something I've fought against my entire life.

Early memories of my worry lead us to a time where I was sitting in my third-grade class in a beanbag next to my teacher. I was afraid of sitting alone, so my teacher actually let me sit next to her desk. I was so consumed with what-ifs. If my parents didn't pick me up on time from school, my mind always shot to the worst-case scenario. What if they got into a car accident? What if someone stole their car and now they can't come get me? I worried so much in elementary school. There was a period when I had developed really bad stomachaches from ulcers that were a result of the constant worry. Worry drove my decisions. Worry told me how to act. Worry ultimately robbed me from ever enjoying being present. As I grew older, my anxieties never fully went away. I feel like I just got busier, which, in all honesty, just resulted in me becoming distracted from a lot of my fears. I became really good at hiding my fears and worries until the day that Karen and I lost Asher. From the moment that I broke down in the car outside the hospital that morning, the walls of pretending like everything's okay came crashing down. This began my journey of confronting my fears. From that moment forward, I started having panic attacks. At the time of them happening, I wasn't entirely sure what was happening. There were times when I felt like I was going to pass out for no reason. I would get light-headed and would feel like I couldn't stand up straight, and I felt an unceasing feeling of feeling unsafe. This happened at times when I was sitting, when I was driving, and even at times when I was preaching. It got so bad that I finally decided to go to the doctor and get my health checked out. Keep in mind, I didn't know it was anxiety that was causing this yet. After the doctor told me that my health was normal, I carried on through life learning to deal with these feelings that wouldn't go away. With each week and month that passed, it felt as though it was getting more and more frequent. This feeling carried over into a trip that Karen and I took to Nashville for a church convention. While we were in Nashville, it's like all my feelings and senses were heightened. I constantly felt off-balanced. I had no appetite the whole time we were there, and I could barely sleep. We traveled to this convention with two of our good friends from our church. On one of the nights before session started, we got some sushi with our friends in the same hotel that the convention was being held at. Our conversation started to hint at our friend feeling some similar things that I was feeling. When I started to ask questions about what they felt, I learned about the term panic attack and how that was causing a lot of what they were struggling with. This conversation led to me being referred to their therapist, which then led to me beginning a deep process of healing. Therapy was truly orchestrated by God. I completely believe that God put that therapist in my life to bring healing. A lot of what I discovered in my sessions was how much of my life was controlled by fear. The what-ifs silently assassinated my mind. The fear and worry continued to wage war in my mind until I was introduced to a new way to look at the what ifs. Two words changed my life forever: even if.

Worry can be truly crippling. I've heard it said before that worry adds a giant shadow to small things. Our present experiences can easily be overshadowed by things that might not even happen. Worry can prevent you from ever stepping into something new. Worry can even rob you of living the life that God gave His Son's life for. When I got the opportunity to interview for youth pastor, my mind was bombarded with what-ifs. What if I'm not good enough? What if I don't know the Bible well enough? What if something happens that

I'm not prepared for? What if I let everyone down? What if I fail? God met me in my doubts and gracefully helped disband each one with two beautiful words: even if. "Even if you feel not good enough, I say you are. Even if you don't know the Bible well enough, My Holy Spirit will give you the words to say when you need to say them. Even if you feel unprepared, I will be with you. Even if you feel as though you've let people down, you will never let Me down. I hold you up." Here's the antidote that will starve even your deepest worries: even if. Two words that can flip fear and worry upside down. When you begin to confront your what-ifs with even ifs, you will soon begin to see how strong you really are. You'll also begin to discover how hollow your worries truly are. From this life to eternity, God has it under control. Even if is a gift that God has given us to fight even our most crippling fears. Even if is rooted in faith, knowing that God is genuinely in control. Even if comes from knowing who God truly is. Romans 8:28 is the promise that fuels even if. It has EASILY become one of my favorite scriptures. It says, "And we know that God causes everything to work together for the good of those who love God and are called according to His purpose for them."

God works ALL things together. Even if something challenging happens, you still have God. In that same chapter of Romans, Paul says the following:

> What shall we say about such wonderful things as these? If God is for us, who can ever be against us? Since He did not spare even His own Son but gave Him up for us all, won't He also give us everything else? Who dares accuse us whom God has chosen for His own? No one...for God Himself has given us right standing with Himself. Who then will condemn us? No one... for Christ Jesus died for us and was raised to life for us, and He is sitting in the place of honor at God's right hand, pleading for us. Can anything ever separate us from Christ's love? Does it

mean He no longer loves us if we have trouble or calamity, or are persecuted, or hungry, or destitute, or in danger, or threatened with death? No, despite all these things, overwhelming victory is ours through Christ, who loved us. And I am convinced that nothing can ever separate us from God's love. Neither death nor life, neither angels nor demons, neither our fears for today nor our worries about tomorrow...not even the powers of hell can separate us from God's love. No power in the sky above or in the earth below...indeed, nothing in all creation will ever be able to separate us from the love of God that is revealed in Christ Jesus our Lord. (Romans 8:31–39)

When you have God on your side, you have everything. This is the confidence that we obtain when we have a relationship with Jesus. God will forever be in our corner no matter what happens. Our circumstances can never dictate that. Even when we go through challenging times, it will never take away God's love from us. No matter how many times we fail, we can never cause God to love us more or less. This is our assurance as believers! This assurance destroys what-ifs and gives us the ability to answer with an even if. This equation changes all our question marks into exclamation marks. We will call the even if mentality as fire insurance.

When I think of the term fire insurance in relation to following Christ, the first thing that pops into my mind are those people that stand on top of the soap boxes in crowded places with megaphones yelling "Turn or burn! Follow Jesus or you will burn in hell for eternity!" Now, what they're saying isn't necessarily false, but I wonder if that level of condemnation has ever pushed someone closer to Jesus? In Romans 2:4, it talks about how God's kindness is intended to turn us toward Him, not push us away from Him. If we look at giving our lives to Jesus simply as a "get out of hell" free pass, we are missing the message in its entirety. Following Jesus not only affects our eternity. It changes everything we know about our lives here on earth as well. Genuine fire insurance is embracing the even if mentality.

In Daniel 3, right before Shadrach, Meshach, and Abednego were thrown into the fire, there was a heated (no pun intended) exchange between them and King Neb. Their response to Neb's threats is EVERYTHING when it comes to facing the fires of oppression. Check it out:

> I will give you one more chance to bow down and worship the statue I have made when you hear the sound of the musical instruments. But if you refuse, you will be thrown immediately into the blazing furnace. And then what god will be able to rescue you from my power? Shadrach, Meshach, and Abednego replied, "O Nebuchadnezzar, we do not need to defend ourselves before you. If we are thrown into the blazing furnace, the God whom we serve is able to save us. He will rescue us from your power, Your Majesty. *But even if He doesn't,* we want to make it clear to you, Your Majesty, that we will never serve your gods or worship the gold statue you have set up." (Daniel 3:15–18, emphasis added)

How POWERFUL is that? Even if He doesn't. Wow. This statement is key to overcoming our fear. In essence, what this is saying is, "We believe that God is able to do anything He wants, but even if He doesn't, we won't compromise our faith in Him." How many of us base our understanding of how much God loves us on how much He does for us? We start to treat God like a genie in a bottle or a celestial sugar daddy and only come to Him when we have a need. What happens when our prayer isn't answered the way we want it to be? How many of us have felt abandoned by God when He doesn't do exactly what we want Him to do when we want Him to do it? Fireproof faith knows that God is good no matter the outcome of our trials. Having this mind-set will give you courage to take on any fire that comes your way. Even if strips away all layers of our fears and cuts straight to the root of what's causing it. An even if mind-set kicks down barriers, hunts down your fears, and stares it straight in the face. I challenge you right now to take a brief break from reading the book and determine what some of your what-ifs are. When you find them, change the vocabulary to even if, and watch that fear be dominated. I'll give you an example before you go on your even if adventure:

I'm afraid of going on a mission trip to Mexico.

"What if I am put in a position where I need to speak? I don't know Spanish."

What this statement is rooted in is a fear of feeling incompetent or unprepared. Rather than letting the fear of failure define you, approach it like this:

"Even if I'm put in a position where I need to speak, even though I don't know Spanish, I know that God will either give me the words to say, or He will put someone there with me that can help me." Boom.

Or how about this scenario:

"What if I get kidnapped in Mexico? That's a real problem, right?"

Taking it there, you can say, "Even if I get kidnapped in Mexico, I know God will protect me. Even if He doesn't deliver me from that situation and the worst scenario happens, like losing my life, I know I will be in paradise with my Heavenly Father forever."

See how even ifs can take the wind out of the sails of even the deepest fear when you sit down with them? Here's the next step to your even if journey: Once you have your even if statements, find some promises in God's Word to anchor them. Like we learned earlier in the book, it's super important to know why you believe what you believe. If you have an even if statement that sounds good but isn't anchored in God's Word, it's just hopeful thinking. You must make sure that your faith statements are anchored. If they aren't anchored, they will be burned up the moment you step foot into the fire.

Whenever you're about to take a step further in your calling, what-ifs always poke their nasty little heads up. Have you noticed that? Maybe our what-ifs can be solid indicators that we are stepping into God's plan for our lives. When you live your life fueled by faith, what-ifs will try to enter into your thought life often.

I'll never forget the time that God called me to leave my band to step into the internship that trained me for ministry. When I was a senior in high school, I started this Christian worship band with a couple of my friends. Long story short, I did that band for four years, and God was all up in it. We recorded two full-length albums and led worship for church services, youth group nights, camps, and retreats. We also had the opportunity to lead worship at a Catholic barbeque once. The MC was a drunk Elvis. Talk about a unique experience. Anyways, God blessed this band. So much so that I was convinced that I was going to do that for the rest of my life. I was in that band for four years after high school, and because it was going so well, I didn't even go to college. I knew that what I was doing was bigger than me and that I was right where I needed to be. These were amazing times. I got to play music with my best friends, which I love to do with my whole heart, and I got to lead people in worship. Nothing was bad or off about anything that was happening. One night, we were practicing in one of the members' grandma's house, like we always did, getting ready for a trip we were about to take to lead worship in Arizona. The rehearsal went well, and as I was sitting in my car about to go home, a thought popped into my mind. This thought was so clear and loud it might as well have been audible. I heard, "Brandon, I want to take our relationship deeper. Are you willing to do that?" Now keep in mind that up to this point in my life, I don't think I've ever heard God speak to me like that, so I wasn't sure what to think of it. I responded in my mind, *God? If that's You, I'm down.* Not fully realizing what I did at the moment, I signed myself up for a crazy, God-fueled adventure. The next week, we had another practice because our trip was quickly approaching. At the conclusion, I was feeling great about the coming Arizona worship set. I knew my parts, both singing and guitar, and felt really confident about them. Not only was the music sounding good, but the guys in the band were all working well together. Nothing beats that moment when members of a team are jiving together. Nothing. As we all said our goodbyes, I made my way to my car and sat for a little before driving home. Just like the week prior, that clear, piercing thought came back. This time, the message was a little more straightforward. "I want you to leave this." This was such a random thought, and let me remind you, these were my best friends. There wasn't an argument or disagreement that spurred on this thought. Everything was going extremely well. We were recording an album and had multiple opportunities to lead worship at different churches. Of course, if I'm about to leave my dream and my best friends, I needed to know that this was God talking to me. Oddly enough, even though that thought was putting into question everything I was working on, I had peace. A couple days after that rehearsal, I sat down and talked with a good friend of mine that was the youth pastor at the church I was attending. As I proceeded to tell him what I was thinking about doing, the moment the words came out of my mouth, his eyes got HUGE. It seemed like they were going to fall out of his face. I thought for a second that I said something that offended him. What I'm about to tell you next is one of those things that truly makes no sense outside of it being a God thing. After I told him I was thinking about leaving the band, he told me that the day prior to me wanting to talk with him, he was driving home, and he had a random thought: "If I (God) were to ask Brandon to leave the band, do you think he would?" Having such a random thought like that, he went home and talked about it with his wife. His wife didn't want him to tell me what he was thinking because she didn't want him to manipulate my decisions in any way. His response to God was, "God, if this is You, You're going to need to tell Brandon Yourself." The moment he said this to me, I was in shock. I was excited, scared, confident, and confused all at the same time. I knew what I needed to do, but I didn't know how I was going to do it. The what-ifs started to flood my mind. "What if my friends won't want to be friends anymore? What if I'm making a wrong decision? What if I'm ruining the one good thing I have going for me?" What-ifs always come in pivotal seasons of your life. In the midst of all the worry and doubt, God's peace continued to propel me forward. The day that I told the guys my plan, I was blown away by their support. At the time, I didn't know what I was going to pursue next. All I knew was I needed to be obedient and leave the band. It, in all honesty, was one of the hardest decisions I've had to make on my own in my entire life. After leaving the band, I felt drawn to an internship program that the church I was going to was talking about starting up. There was no degrees promised and no licenses promised. It was to simply take your relationship with God deeper. Looking back on God's original question to me, I knew that this is what I needed to do. Not knowing this at the time, that internship was going to be the thing that opened up the door for me to step into youth pastoring at a different church. The internship was a three-year, youth-focused, intensive program that trained up people in how to pastor and lead a ministry. There was graphic design, sermon prep, life lessons, and even workouts. At the end of the three years, after working on staff at the church for a short season, the opportunity to step into youth pastoring fell into my lap.

I was going back and forth with whether to share this part of the story in its entirety here, but I really do want you to get a sense of how interested God is in the details of our lives and how crippling what-ifs can be if you allow them be.

So my mom does nails. She's done nails for as long as I can remember. As a result of this, I know more about manicures and pedicures than most men on this planet do. One day, toward the end of the day, I get a call from my mom. As soon as I pick up the phone, she starts talking a million miles a minute. She was beyond ecstatic. She was telling me how she just met this lady and her daughter and that the lady and her husband pastor a local church, and they were looking for a youth pastor! "Are you interested?!" my mom threw out there. Without any hesitation, my response was, "Nope! Thanks though! Have a good night." And we hung up the phone.

"Brandon, don't you youth pastor now?" You might be thinking to yourself. If that's what you were thinking, you are correct. Now, my internship was focused on youth. I loved the youth, but I definitely didn't want to be the one responsible for the youth. Youth ministry is HARD. Most of the time, it feels like they don't like you. That feeling of people not liking you isn't the most sought-after feeling in my mind. I would serve in a youth ministry, but ask me to lead it and I'll respectfully decline. As soon as I hung up the phone with my mom, it felt like I was sucker punched in the stomach. I knew I needed to call her back and get more information in regards to the opportunity. Right before I called her back, the what-ifs began. "What if I'm not good enough? What if they don't like me? What if I don't have enough experience? What if I end up really wanting the position and they give it to someone else?" They were unbearable. In spite of the doubt, I picked up my phone and called my mom back to get all the information. That phone call led to another phone interview, which led to a lunch interview, which led to the opportunity to speak to their youth, which led to a job offer, which led to a position that I've been in for over five years. There were what-ifs around every single corner. My insecurities were amplified, and my doubts were on display. At the end of the day, the even ifs outweighed the what-ifs, and I slowly inched forward into my calling. I love every moment of youth pastoring.

If only we became more aware of our what-ifs. It's as if the what-ifs are a sign that God's about to do something amazing in your life. The next time you feel a what-if creep in, take a step back and interrogate that sucker. Like the Bible says, take that bad boy captive. Not like a "Hey, what's your name? Please don't mess with me" kind of questioning. I'm talking like a Jack Bauer, "you've just caught some terrorist that's about to destroy your life so you're going to kick them in the freaking face" kind of questioning. Boldly capture that thought and see it for what it is—a preview of the glory that's about to be poured out into your life. If you're not having any what-ifs, it's time to start taking some bold steps deeper into God's calling for your life.

The Bible is full of incredible individuals who accomplished epic things all the while combating the what-ifs. In the Old Testament, there's a guy named Moses. The book of Exodus, the second book of the Bible, is surrounding the story of when God's people, who were under Egyptian rule, broke free from their slavery in Egypt and went forward to a land that God had promised them. Moses was the individual that God handpicked to lead His people out of their oppression. Here's the thing though, after God had spoken to Moses and called him to do this epic thing, Moses started arguing with God and began sifting through his own personal what-ifs. Here's how it went down. Moses was tending to some of his father-in-law's sheep in the wilderness when, all of a sudden, God started speaking to him through a bush that was on fire. If you've ever heard of a burning bush moment, this is where it originates from. God caught Moses' attention and commissioned him to be the one to set God's people free. Here's how the exchange between Moses and God unfolded. Keep an eye out for how Moses started to sift through his what-ifs:

> Then the Lord told him, "I have certainly seen the oppression of my people in Egypt. I have heard their cries of distress because of their harsh slave drivers. Yes, I am aware of their suffering. So I have come down to rescue them from the power of the Egyptians and lead them out of Egypt into their own fertile and spacious land. It is a land flowing with milk and honey…the land where the Canaanites, Hittites, Amorites, Perizzites, Hivites, and Jebusites now live. Look! The cry of the people of Israel has reached me, and I have seen how harshly the Egyptians abuse them. Now go, for I am sending you to Pharaoh. You must lead my people Israel out of Egypt." But Moses protested to God. "Who am I to appear before Pharaoh? Who am I to lead the people of Israel out of Egypt?" God answered, "I will be with

you. And this is your sign that I am the one who has sent you: When you have brought the people out of Egypt, you will worship God at this very mountain." But Moses protested, "If I go to the people of Israel and tell them, 'The God of your ancestors has sent me to you,' they will ask me, 'What is His name?' Then what should I tell them?" God replied to Moses, "I AM WHO I AM. Say this to the people of Israel: I AM has sent me to you." (Exodus 3:7–12)

Here's the what-if progression: God called, Moses argued, God affirmed and encouraged. This is the same cycle that we all go through in our lives now. What-ifs are always founded on how we perceive ourselves to be. Even ifs are always founded in the truth of who God is. The more we focus on self, the more we fuel our what-ifs. The more we focus on God and His faithfulness, the more we fuel our even ifs. Focusing on God gives us a refreshed perspective, and it's that perspective that can propel us forward into the calling that God has for us. If the goals and dreams you have for your life don't cause you to pause and ask the question "What am I about to get myself into?" I guarantee it's not a God-sized dream. What is it that you want to accomplish in your life? What are the things that are in your heart that you want to see happen? Things that seem impossible to do in your own strength and ability? Notice how whenever you start to take steps to accomplish those dreams, what-ifs always come up. Again, if you have what-ifs, you're probably going in the right direction. Moses eventually stepped up and stepped into the calling God had for his life. With each step he took, God was not only right there beside him, it was obvious that God had already gone before him and made his path straight.

There are so many examples throughout the Bible of people receiving a word, dream, or vision from God for their lives that seemed impossible. The more they focused on their own ability, the more discouraged and defeated they felt. When they finally took their eyes off the what-ifs and began to stand in the even ifs, that's when the breakthrough started to happen. Could it be that the breakthrough you're desiring in your life today is patiently waiting for you to walk away from the what-ifs and to boldly step into the even ifs? The more we operate in the even ifs, the less focused we are on the outcome of things. If we are so focused on the outcome, we begin to place God into a box. We begin to think that if God doesn't do what we are expecting Him to do, it must mean that He doesn't love us or He doesn't care about us. In life, at least in my life, I've noticed that things don't happen the way I want them to. The tighter we hold on to our situations, the more painful they tend to be. When we surrender them to the Lord in faith, we begin to sense God's peace. Faith is all about letting go of your desired results. Of course, God wants us to desire things and want things, but at the end of the day, if we don't want to be consumed with fears, concerns, or anxieties, we must decide that God is more important than any of it.

If we want to make it through the fire, we must stand on and confess our even ifs. If we want to confess the even ifs, we must master the art of surrender. Surrender is a topic that I personally have a hard time with. I like to be in control of my life. I like to have a say in the things that happen. But the more I go through life, the more I realize that we can't really control anything. The more we try to control, the more hurt we allow in. When you err on the side of control, you're neglecting both the what-ifs and even ifs. When the what-ifs become so overwhelming, if you don't step into the even ifs, control is an automatic response that kicks in. In order to transfer from what if to even if without control, you must embrace surrender. Surrender is scary because it's literally giving up control. Surrender is the bridge that we must walk on to get to the even ifs. I'm pretty sure that Jesus didn't want to die on a cross, but HE did it anyways because He lived His life surrendered to God's will. The cross, in case you didn't know, was a torture device that the Romans used to put the worst of the worst criminals to death. Death by means of crucifixion was the most painful and brutal way to die. Not only was it physically shameful, but it was spiritually shameful as well.

The individual who was going to die by means of crucifixion would first be stripped naked. After they were completely naked in front of people, they would receive a whipping or lashes from a whip that had glass tips or nails. They would be whipped thirty-nine times or until your internal organs were exposed, whichever one happened first. After this scourging, as they called it, you would then need to pick up your own wooden cross and carry it yourself to the place of your crucifixion. If you survived that journey, you would then be attached to your cross using seven-inch nails. These nails would be driven through both your wrists and heels. These were the nails that would hold you up once the cross was put upright with you on it. The longer you hung on the cross, the harder it became to breathe. If you needed to catch your breath, you would need to put all your weight on your heels and pull up with your wrists, which was excruciating. If the prisoner, by chance, survived three whole days, the officer would then come and break their knees so they couldn't lift themselves anymore. This was considered mercy. This is what Jesus went through for you and for me.

Knowing this was the fire He was about to step in to, Jesus pleaded with God right before He got arrested. Look at how it unfolded:

> "Father, if You are willing, please take this cup of suffering away from me. Yet I want Your will to be done, not mine." Then an angel from Heaven appeared and strengthened Him. He prayed more fervently, and He was in such agony of spirit that His sweat fell to the ground like great drops of blood. (Luke 22:42–43)

No matter how much Jesus didn't want to endure the cross, He chose to surrender His desires and fulfill God's will. This is the greatest example of an even if mentality. Can you imagine how many what-ifs crossed Jesus's mind during this entire experience? The what-ifs became a reality for Him, and He made it through it. God came through. God always comes through. It just might not look the way we want it to. Once we let go of our desires to make it happen our own way, God is free to walk us through the fire and work miracles.

Isaiah 55:8–9 says, "'My thoughts are nothing like your thoughts,' says the Lord. 'And my ways are far beyond anything you could imagine. For just as the Heavens are higher than the earth, so my ways are higher than your ways and my thoughts higher than your thoughts.'" The sooner we accept this to be true, the sooner we will be fireproof. God's methods are truly different than our methods. My genuine prayer is that this book is a source of hope and comfort for people who are hurting. Who knows if I ever would have found the motivation to start writing it had we never gone through the loss of our baby? An even if mentality safeguards your faith in God because it takes the results out of the equation. Results are nice, of course, but the picture is so much bigger than just the end product. God is all about the process while we are here on earth. The process is messy, irritating at times, and long, but the sooner we embrace the even ifs, the sooner we can step into this incredible journey that God has laid before us. The fire is a necessary part of the process, and we are able to make it through the fire if, and only if, we have an even if mentality.

VALLEY

The Lord is my best friend and my shepherd. I always have more than enough. He offers a resting place for me in His luxurious love. His tracks take me to an oasis of peace, the quiet brook of bliss. That's where He restores and revives my life. He opens before me pathways to God's pleasure and leads me along in His footsteps of righteousness so that I can bring honor to His name. Lord, even when your path takes me THROUGH the valley of deepest darkness, fear will never conquer me, for You already have! You remain close to me and lead me THROUGH it all the way. Your authority is my strength and my peace. The comfort of Your love takes away my fear. I'll never be lonely, for You are near. (Psalm 23:1–4 TPT)

Storms and fires aren't the only things that people go through in life. The valley is something that everyone experiences, and ironically enough, they would have no idea that they're going through it. The storm is loud, violent, and aggressive. It shakes you to your core. The fire is painful, excruciating, and strips us down to the purest form of who we are. The valley is, by far, neither one of those. The valley is quiet, cold, lonely, and in my opinion, extremely challenging to walk through. Join me as we enter into our final stretch of our through journey.

10

THE IN-BETWEEN

There's something about the great outdoors that refreshes the soul. That breath of fresh air that gets the blood pumping. If I'm being completely honest, I'll take Netflix over going outside any day (don't judge me). Netflix has some riveting documentaries about nature. Some of them are even narrated by Morgan Freeman. Nothing is more soothing than the sound of Morgan Freeman teaching you about global warming. When I'm all caught up with my Netflix shows though, I do love being in nature. It's so simple to clear your head in nature. There's something about God's uninterrupted creation that draws you in. People love the mountains. People love the beach. Which do you like more? You're either a mountain person or a beach person. If you're both, you're called a Californian. Look, I know that the stereotypical Californian is the surfer bum type (cha bra, tubular type of person), but if you really think about it, a Californian can go surfing and snowboarding in the same day. California for the win. For me, I'll take the beach over the mountains any day. When I go to the beach, I love to have a Starbucks in one hand and a good book to read in the other. You won't ever catch me actually going into the water in a California beach. It literally blows me away when I see people enjoying being in water that's slightly above freezing. Sure, it's enjoyable…after you become numb and lose all sensation in your limbs. The beach in Guatemala, on the other hand, is a WHOLE different story. The water isn't too cold, and it isn't too hot. It's PERFECT. Not to mention that the sand in Guatemala is black. So cool. I do love the beach, way more than mountains, but there's nothing quite like the silence that comes from being on top of a mountain with no one around. Clean mountain air is truly so refreshing. There's actually a lot you can do in the mountains when you really think about it. Hiking is one of those things that I enjoy most about being in the mountains. Let me tell you, I've had some pretty memorable hiking experiences in my life. Back in the day, when I was serving as an internship director, at the end of one of the intern years, I wanted to take the interns to a mountaintop and have this epic experience where they sat and journaled about the whole year. I had it all mapped out. All the details were falling into place, except for this major detail: I had no idea where we were going to go hiking. The Saturday before our calendared trip, my friend Thomas and I went adventuring in the mountains to try and find the perfect spot. I had an idea in my mind as to what I wanted the spot to be like. Things like having a good view at the end of the hike, multiple paths to take, etc. You know, life-applicable examples. Thomas and I literally drove around for four hours in the mountains looking for the right spot, and we found nothing. The only pull offs that we saw were super lame. We were about to give up and go home when the desire to drive for five more minutes welled up. Thank God we did. We drove just a tad bit more, and around one of the turns, we stumbled upon, in my opinion, one of the most perfect hiking spots ever. There was a legitimate trail head that was at the beginning of this epic location. Thomas and I wanted to, of course, scope it out first. We were so excited. There was everything you could imagine in this one spot. There were amazing views, tunnels that went through the mountain, pathways that curved every which way, and to top it all off, there is an epic mountaintop experience (literally). It took us about forty minutes to make it, but when we did, it was so worth it. At the top of this mountain were handmade benches, telescopes that pointed in the direction of multiple other mountaintops, and a spot that was cleared out that was perfect for taking pictures. When Thomas and I made it to the top, we were ecstatic. It was everything I'd ever imagined it being. As we were running around the top of this mountain, something started to shift. The shifting wasn't happening on the mountain. Rather, the shifting was happening on my insides. Have you ever gotten so excited for something that it made you want to poop? Yep. This is what was happening to me. I was so pumped about finding this mountaintop that this excitement sped up my metabolizing process. I started to panic. The sweats were real. I didn't know what I was going to do. Was I going to hold it? Has this ever happened to you? There are times when this sensation hits you and you're able to hold it. This was not one of those times. Mother Nature was calling me, and she was NOT letting me ignore her calls. I had only one choice. Keep in mind, it was just me and Thomas on top of this mountain. I asked Tom to take a walk so I could spend some alone time in the bushes. Let's just say there was Mountain Dew on top of that mountain, and we didn't have any soda. ANYWAYS!

Life is full of mountaintop experiences. Maybe not as literal as the story I just shared with you, but you know the term. When you experience a moment that's incredible, that's a mountaintop moment. It's like you're bulletproof. Nothing can shake you, and nothing can touch you. As a youth pastor, I am all too familiar with the mountaintop experience that happens in the students at camp. They are there, away from their phones, away from the day-to-day drama, with the sole purpose to grow closer with their church friends and to grow closer with God and have an experience with Him. I've seen it so many times, where these kids have an AMAZING experience up at camp, life-changing experiences. The last message that's preached at camps every single time is the "What are you going to do when you come off of the mountain?" message. Mountaintop moments are amazing, but they are ALWAYS followed by a valley. Have you noticed that? After you experience something amazing, it's only a matter of time until something happens to knock you down off the mountaintop. When you come down off the mountain, you now find yourself in the valley.

Valleys, by definition, are low areas of land between hills or mountains. Valleys typically have streams or rivers running through them. Simply put, valleys are the in-between. They come in between the mountaintop moments, and they are LOW. In storms, you're tossed around, beat up, and shaken to your core. Storms cause you to ask the question "Am I going to make it through this?" Everyone goes through storms. It's not a matter of *if* you will go through a storm. It's *when*. Fires are reserved for those who make the personal decision to follow Jesus. Fires of oppression, though they are challenging, cleanse you, free you, and purify you. Fires cause you to ask the question "Is this truly worth it?" Valleys, compared to storms and fires, are totally different. Valleys are dark and quiet, and if I had to pick a word that summarizes what my impression of a valley is, it would be lonely. They cause you to ask the question "Am I alone?" Valleys are lonely. Valleys are depressing. Storms, fires, and mountaintops are all moments. They come, and they go. Valleys, I've noticed, are more like seasons. They are the extended time that follows storms, fires, and mountaintop moments. They are the in-between. These are the times when you really start to battle with your inner self. Mine and Karen's mountaintop moment came the moment we found out we were pregnant for the first time. It was truly a high. Nothing felt real. It was euphoric. The storm happened when we found out that we lost the baby, and that storm straight up knocked me on my butt. It swept the rug out from right underneath my feet. As the dust gradually settled from the storm, I found myself feeling more alone than ever. I was in my own personal valley. I looked behind me and saw in the distance the cloudy silhouettes of our mountaintop moments. If I squinted really hard, I could vaguely make out the silhouette of mountaintop moments to come. But what about the valley I was in? It felt like every time I yelled out for help, I only heard a faint echo of my own voice. This is the valley. I think a lot of us find ourselves in the valley and aren't even aware of it. The valley can be called an off day or feeling tired all of the time, or you can even call it depression. After we lost Asher, I really did fall into a deep depression. If you asked me at the time if I considered myself depressed, I would have probably said no, but looking back, I was severely depressed. I had no motivation to get out of bed. I didn't want to talk to anybody, see anybody, or spend time with anybody. I didn't want to go to church, let alone preach messages about things I wasn't even sure I still believed. I was sad from the moment I woke up in the morning to the time when I went to sleep. I was feeling sad even before anything happened that could have caused sadness. It was a very dark time. No matter how many people I was physically around with, I couldn't shake the feeling of being alone. I was truly alone in a crowded room. The valley is the moment that comes between the massacre and the miracle. Jesus was killed on a Friday and resurrected on a Sunday. What happened on the Saturday?

After Jesus took His final breaths on the cross on that Friday, His disciples, the ones who spent every day with Him, were scattered. Peter, one of the closest disciples to Jesus, denied that he even knew Jesus just days prior. Imagine the guilt he felt after finding out that his rabbi and friend was murdered moments after he lied about knowing Him. Jesus showed nothing but unconditional love and favor toward Peter, and how does Jesus get thanked? Peter pretended that he didn't even KNOW HIM. For three years, these disciples spent every moment with Jesus. They gave up everything to follow Him. They left their families, their traditions, and their jobs and devoted every part of who they were to being with Jesus. They followed Him, learned from Him, and mimicked the very things that He did. They were His students. Life, as they knew it, was now drastically different after the cross. Talk about a storm, and talk about a valley. Many of us are in a continual state of Saturday. Friday happened and rocked us, and we haven't experienced Sunday yet. We know and have hope that Sunday is coming, but we are still in Saturday. Maybe you're in Saturday right now. Maybe you've been in Saturday for a long time now. Though it's quiet and sometimes scary, I want you to know that you're not alone.

There's a story in John 11 when two of Jesus's close friends, Mary and Martha, experience a terrible storm. At the point of this story, Mary and Martha send word to Jesus and ask Him to come visit them to heal their brother and also His friend, Lazarus, because he was deathly ill. When Jesus got word about their request, rather than going right away, the Bible says that He stayed behind where He was (verse 6). Have you ever felt like God was late in answering your requests? Though I'm all too familiar with the feeling, the truth is that He is never late. In the time between Mary and Martha reaching out to Jesus and Jesus arriving to them, their brother, Lazarus, passed away. Two times Mary and Martha say to Jesus, "If only you had been here, my brother would not have died." They were in the valley. If you know the story, you know that Jesus shows up, raises Lazarus from the dead, crazy miracle goes down, and people freak out praise God. Everything's amazing, but there was a period between the death and the resurrection. This period was the valley. Valleys are a painful and very real part of the process.

For someone that's impatient like me, the valley can be an excruciating experience. Earlier this year in 2020, we experienced something that none of us in our lifetimes have ever experienced. We were introduced to a sickness that goes by the name COVID-19, a new strain of the coronavirus. I know coronavirus was a thing before 2020, but I honestly had no idea what it was. When COVID started spreading rapidly throughout the world, many countries made the decision to go into lockdown. Here in America, we were given instructions to stay at home and only go out for necessary things. The quarantine of 2020 had begun. One week turned to two, and two eventually turned to six. People had thought that it was only going to last a couple of weeks, but life as we knew it before quarantine still isn't a reality as I write this. In the future, when I think back to living through the pandemic, I'll remember not being able to buy toilet paper, watching *Tiger King*, and learning how to make whipped coffee. Those three things will forever summarize the COVID-19 quarantine for me. During the quarantine, people were picking up new hobbies to help pass their time while staying home. Some picked up cooking, while others started new at-home workout routines. For me, I started to sell Pokémon cards on eBay. Just before the safer-at-home instructions were given, I started to go through a bunch of my old things from my dad's house. He and my stepmom were starting to reorganize a lot of things, so it was a perfect opportunity for me to start rummaging through my old things. In the midst of all the yo-yos and beanie babies were two binders stacked with Pokémon cards. These were GOLD. Prior to this, I had never sold anything on eBay. My stepbrothers were really into it, but I never found the motivation to learn how to do it. For fun, I busted out eBay to look up how much one of my Pokémon cards was worth. This wasn't just any plain card. This was a holographic Charizard card that was in immaculate condition. I found a bunch of them for sale on eBay and figured why not? The worst thing that could happen is that it doesn't sell, right? I snapped some pictures of it and threw it up online. Literally, within minutes, I was receiving offers and bids for the card. It BLEW UP. By the end of the seven-day auction, the card sold for close to $165. Yeah. I know, right? This experience ignited a passion for selling old things on eBay. You could say that it became my quarantine side hustle. I was slinging Pokémon cards and yo-yos left and right. The whole experience is really entertaining, except for one part of the process. I literally LOATHE waiting for my item to make it to the person who purchased it. There have been times when the item I sold stopped providing updates on the tracking, and it was delivered weeks after the original estimated delivery date. Freakin' COVID. The waiting is terrible. The not knowing is terrible. This same impatience translates to my everyday life as well, and you better believe it bleeds over into how mine and God's relationship is. The in-between is so hard for me because in the moments of waiting, it's so easy to become anxious. The pressures of where you came from to where you're going can make the process so stressful. Months after we lost Asher, there was a turning point in my heart that changed everything about my perspective of the valley.

I remember lying in bed one night, not able to fall asleep, just staring up at the point where the ceiling met the wall. I could barely see anything because I didn't have my glasses on, and if you know me, you know that my eyes are terrible. I can't see ANYTHING without my contacts or glasses. Karen had already fallen asleep, and Dallas, our dog, was sleeping under the covers in between my legs. Fun fact about Dallas: he always burrows under the covers to sleep. I guess it's a dachshund thing. In the stillness and quietness of that moment, my mind started to race. Literally all at once, I was bombarded with memories of that day in February. I started to feel overwhelmed, so I started to cry. At this point in time, Karen and I had started to try to get pregnant again and weren't able to. I'm stuck in the middle of two mountaintops: the moment when we were pregnant before and when I hope for us to be pregnant again. I'm fighting thoughts of doubt, fear, anger, and worry, and in the midst of it all, there was suddenly a great calm. It was like one of those scenes from a movie where the character gets swept away to another dimension and they are in a large white room. I was there in my mind. In the midst of the bombardment of thoughts, a still, small voice slipped in and said, "Breathe." I took a deep breath in and let the deep breath out. Something about that breath slowed down time. In and out. In and out. With every breath out, it was as if I was letting go of my concerns. Amazing how, genuinely, one encounter with God can give you the strength you need to get through the valley. The valley can be a beautiful place the moment you stop being consumed with the mountaintops behind you and in front of you. Be present, because God's presence is with you in the valley. Enjoy every minute you've been given to live. The moment you start to appreciate the valley, that's the moment when your healing begins.

The power of presence is something that is so easily overlooked. There are so many people around us that are there physically but are mentally in a totally different place. The valley is a place that you can be present in. "Stop and smell the roses" is a line that we've all heard before but something that holds a truth so profound it can change your life. It's so easy to be consumed by memories of past mountaintop experiences and mountaintop experiences that we desire still to come that we miss out on the beauty that surrounds us in the valley today. One word is key if we want to master the art of being present—contentment. It's so rare to meet someone in our day and age who is genuinely content. To be clear, contentment is not complacency or laziness. Simply put, contentment is being at peace with who you are and what you have in your life. The valley can create restlessness in us when we start thinking about what we don't have. I can't even begin to tell you how much sleep I lose at the thought of the things I was never going to experience with Asher. I was never going to teach him to ride a bike, I was never going to see him play with his grandparents, I was never going to play catch with him at the park, and I was never going to be able to give him my guitar and watch him learn how to play his first songs. The thoughts of what I was going to not have were absolutely crippling. In the middle of all that though, I felt God gently remind me of what I do have. I have an incredible wife, an awesome church, a healthy family, and a roof over my head, and I do believe that one day we will have a baby here on earth. The moment I accepted the reality of the situation and shift my focus to thankfulness instead of bitterness, my perspective of the valley started to change.

There's a famous Bible verse in the book of Philippians 4 that I'm sure you've heard before: "For I can do all things through Christ, who strengthens me" (Philippians 4:13) You'll see this verse on Instagram biographies, bumper stickers, athlete attire, you know. It's pretty epic to think that you can accomplish everything you set your mind to through Jesus's power. Except that's not really what the verse is saying. Of course, I believe that nothing is impossible for God, but that verse doesn't mean that the moment you post it on your bio, you're going to get everything you want. Life doesn't work like that. Instead, let's read that verse in its full context. Also, keep in mind that Paul is writing this FROM JAIL:

> How I praise the Lord that you are concerned about me again. I know you have always been concerned for me, but you didn't have the chance to help me. Not that I was ever in need, For I have learned how to be content with whatever I have. I know how to live on almost nothing or with everything. I have learned the secret of living in every situation, whether it is with a full stomach or empty, with plenty or little. For I can do everything through Christ, who gives me strength. (Philippians 4:10–13)

Crazy how adding three more verses can change the entire meaning of a single verse. What Paul is saying, in a sense, is that being content with Jesus and Jesus alone is key to making it through anything. When you realize that you already have all you need, it releases you from the curse of discontentment. Of course, Karen and

I have a deep desire to have a baby, but in complete honesty, we are content with what the Lord has blessed us with. The moment you find this contentment is the moment you are set free.

One thing I've noticed about life with God while here on earth is that it's less about the destination as it is about the journey getting there. Of course, the destinations are really epic, but a majority of the memories are formed while on the journey. There are a TON of examples in Jesus's life involving Him having life-changing encounters with people while He was on His way somewhere else. When Jesus healed the woman with a chronic issue of bleeding, He was actually on His way somewhere else. When Jesus encountered the Samaritan woman at the well, they were just passing through. In each of these scenarios, the women completely had their lives changed. The woman with the issue of blood had tried for YEARS to get healing from doctors, only to be let down time and time again. Someone that had the condition that she did shouldn't have even gone outside to interact with other people, they were considered to be unclean because of the blood. She went out to a crowd that had gathered around Jesus, fought her way through to Him, and grabbed the tip of His robe. Instantly she was healed. The woman at the well was just as scandalous an encounter. Jews and Samaritans did NOT get along. Jesus and His disciples were Jews, and the woman was a Samaritan. The fact that Jesus and His disciples went through Samaria to get to their destination was already unexpected. On top of all the social expectations being broken, the woman that was getting her water from the well was only there at that time because she didn't want to go out when other people were there. She was living in sin and had numerous failed marriages. So much shame surrounded her. Jesus went out of His way to have an encounter with her, which resulted in her life being changed forever. Jesus showed her love, grace, and compassion, which resulted in her running back to her town and telling everyone there that she could that she encountered the Savior. Both of these moments happened during the journey, not the destination.

The journey of the valley is also FULL of teaching moments. A majority of the things we learn from Jesus's words recorded in the Gospels are teaching moments that came up along the way. Peter

walking on water happened while they were crossing a lake. When Jesus fed five thousand men and their families with only two fish and five loaves of bread also happened unplanned. My question to you is, how many beautiful life experiences are you missing out on because you're too consumed with the mountaintop moments you either have had in the past or desire to have in the future? The more we fantasize about the past or future, the more disconnected we are from being present. Being present is something that's extremely challenging to do in our day and age. Have you noticed that? Whenever Karen and I go out to dinner, we ALWAYS see families sitting together but are not present because they are all on their phones. Smartphones are cool and all, but they destroy our ability to be present. While we are at places physically, the phone allows us to be somewhere else entirely mentally. I can't even tell you how many times I see kids check out in church when I'm giving a message from the pulpit. I see their heads down, and I see that ominous blue glow on their faces that is all too telling of what they are doing. Whether it's TikTok, Instagram, or Minecraft, they aren't present, and I can guarantee that they won't be able to receive what God wants to give them in that moment.

One thing that I noticed for me while I was in the valley was a temptation to find things to distract me from my feelings. I would do just about anything to forget the fact that I was going through a valley. I would get games on my phone and start binge watching shows on Netflix. I would even try to go on more bike rides, anything to get my mind occupied. Here's the problem with that though. Even if I'm physically present in the valley, I won't experience God's presence unless I'm fully present emotionally and mentally as well. Not only will I not experience God's presence if I'm distracted. I also won't begin to heal. Healing doesn't begin until you make the decision to move past bitterness. The valley is ultimately a journey of healing, but only if you want to.

In the book of Genesis, there's a story of two brothers, Jacob and Esau. Jacob and Esau were twins, and like any typical brothers would, they had a bit of a rivalry thing going on. I'm an only child, so the whole sibling rivalry battle doesn't make complete sense. Their rivalry was so intense the Bible even says that they fought each other in their mother's womb (Genesis 25:22). Jacob was a mamma's boy who was quiet tempered. Esau, on the other hand, was favored by his father and loved to hunt and be outdoors. This rivalry continued on through what we read of most of their lives. Culturally, around this time, it was customary for the father to give a blessing to the firstborn son. Even though Jacob and Esau were twins, Esau was born first, so therefore, he was going to be the recipient of his father's blessing. Nearing the end of his life, their dad, Isaac, was preparing to give Esau his blessing. Keeping this in mind, I'm about to share with you something that Jacob did to steal that blessing right out from Esau. To get the full picture of the swindling that's about to go down, I want you to read it straight from the scripture:

> One day when Isaac was old and turning blind, he called for Esau, his older son, and said, "My son," "Yes, Father?" Esau replied. "I am an old man now," Isaac said, "and I don't know when I may die. Take your bow and a quiver full of arrows, and go out into the open country to hunt some wild game for me. Prepare my favorite dish, and bring it here for me to eat. Then I will pronounce the blessing that belongs to you, my firstborn son, before I die." But Rebekah (his wife) overheard what Isaac had said to his son Esau. So when Esau left to hunt for the wild game, she said to her son Jacob, "Listen, I overheard your father say to Esau, 'Bring me some wild game and prepare me a delicious meal. Then I will bless you in the LORD'S presence before I die.' Now, my son, listen to me. Do exactly as I tell you. Go out to the flocks, and bring me two fine young goats. I'll use them to prepare your father's favorite dish. Then take the food to your father so he can eat it and bless you before he dies." (Genesis 27:1–10)

So here's what happens. While Esau was out doing what his dad asked him to do, Jacob dresses up like Esau, pretends to be Esau, brings his dad some of his favorite food, and then asks for the blessing. Isaac, their dad, was super old and super blind, so Jacob and his mom's plan worked. Isaac give Jacob the blessing instead of Esau. When Esau finally came back with the food his dad asked for, looking for that blessing, his dad started to freak out. Very soon after that, they both realized that Jacob tricked them both into stealing Esau's blessing. That's also the type of thing that can't be reversed. What's done is done.

Isaac began to tremble uncontrollably and said, "then who just served me wild game? I have already eaten it, and I blessed him just before you came. And yes, that blessing must stand!" When Esau heard his father's words, he let out a loud and bitter cry. "Oh, my father, what about me? Bless me, too!" he begged. But Isaac said, "Your brother was here, and he tricked me. He has taken away your blessing." Esau exclaimed, "No wonder his name is Jacob, for now he has cheated me twice. First, he took my rights as the firstborn, and now he has stolen my blessing. Oh, haven't you saved even one blessing for me?" Isaac said to Esau, "I have made Jacob your master and have declared that all his brothers will be his servants. I have guaranteed him an abundance of grain and wine...what is left for me to give you, my son?" Esau pleaded, "But do you have only one blessing? Oh, my father, bless me, too!" Then Esau broke down and wept. Finally, his father, Isaac, said to him, "You will live away from the richness of the earth, and away from the dew of the heaven above. You will live by your sword, and you will serve your brother. But when

you decide to break free, you will shake his yoke
from your neck." (Genesis 27:33–40)

How sad is that for Esau? I mean, picture this: he's doing everything he's supposed to be doing. He's following his father's instructions, being a good son. Meanwhile, his brother is home stealing his
blessing! Have you ever felt like that before? You're doing everything
you know you need to do, following God's words and instructions
to the best of your ability. Meanwhile, someone else is getting the
blessing? I can't imagine how upset and betrayed Esau felt. When
Jacob found out that Esau was back, he took off running. This story
is one of the last times we hear of Esau for a while. After this chapter of Genesis concludes, we begin to follow the life of Jacob. Time
goes on, and we begin to learn about Jacob's wife and children. We
literally hear nothing about Esau until Genesis 32. Though it's only
five chapters, we learn that around twenty years passed before Jacob
and Esau encountered each other again. Now THAT is a long valley.
Esau had every reason to be bitter at his brother. He had a lot of time
to be plotting his revenge on Jacob. At least, that's what I would do.
I would spend a ton of time planning out the details as to how I was
going to strike back. (I have problems. Pray for me.) This is exactly
what Jacob was expecting as well. We see in Genesis 32 how Jacob
was sending gifts ahead of them to the place that Esau was living. He
even told his messengers to say things like "Humble greetings from
your servant, Jacob" (Genesis 32:4). He was officially kissing up to
Esau. Gosh, I would too if I ticked off and cheated my brother like
that. The entirety of chapter thirty-two is literally Jacob planning
how he will survive an attack from Esau. He's keeping half of his
possessions protected, he's asking God for mercy, and he's officially
pooping himself. When they finally came in contact with each other,
what happened was truly something unexpected. Check this out:

> Then Jacob looked up and saw Esau coming
> with his 400 men. So, he divided the children
> among Leah, Rachel, and his two servant wives.
> He put the servant wives and their children at

the front, Leah and her children next, and Rachel
and Joseph last. Then Jacob went on ahead. As he
approached his brother, he bowed to the ground
seven times before him. Then Esau ran to meet
him and embraced him, threw his arms around
his neck, and kissed him. And they both wept.
(Genesis 33:1–4)

That doesn't seem like a response from someone that's consumed with bitterness and revenge. Esau, instead of trying to kill
Jacob for what he did, embraced him. Esau, no doubt, went straight
into a valley after the betrayal from Jacob. Anyone with human emotions would. We don't know details about what the valley looked like
for Esau, but what we do know is that he was healed in the valley.
Though the valley can be a lonely season, I've noticed that loneliness
can eventually cause us to lean into God's presence. God's presence
is truly healing. Just being with Him can cause the most broken of
hearts to mend. It's God's presence that leads us through the healing
process of the valley.

No matter how alone you feel in the valley, God is present with
you. That's actually a key factor in getting through the valley, realizing that you're not alone.

Psalm 23 is the passage of scripture that is the foundation for
the idea of going through the valley. It is truly a beautiful psalm. This
particular psalm is written by King David. I can picture David lying
down in the middle of a field, on a break from watching his sheep,
and penning out this poem. Though we opened up this section of
the book with it, let's throw it in here again and really spend some
time digesting it. I'll write it here in The Passion Translation, because
I LOVE the way it flows:

The Lord is my best friend and my shepherd. I
always have more than enough. He offers a resting place for me in His luxurious love. His tracks
take me to an oasis of peace, the quiet brook of
bliss. That's where He restores and revives my life.

He opens before me pathways to God's pleasure and leads me along in His footsteps of righteousness so that I can bring honor to His name. Lord, even when your path takes me THROUGH the valley of deepest darkness, fear will never conquer me, for You already have! You remain close to me and lead me THROUGH it all the way. Your authority is my strength and my peace. The comfort of Your love takes away my fear. I'll never be lonely, for You are near. You become my delicious feast even when my enemies dare to fight. You anoint me with the fragrance of Your Holy Spirit; You give me all I can drink of You until my heart overflows. So why would I fear the future? For your goodness and love pursue me all the days of my life. Then afterward, when my life is through, I'll return to Your glorious presence to be forever with You. (Psalm 23 TPT)

Just let that sink in for a little. WOW.

Sometimes in life, the pathway that we are walking on leads us through a valley. How does David say he makes it through the valleys of life that he goes through? God's presence. In the New Living Translation, it says, "Even when I walk through the darkest valley, I will not be afraid, for You are close beside me" (Psalm 23:4).

We are able to walk through the valley because of God's presence. David says in Psalm 16:11, "You make known to me the path of life; in Your presence there is fullness of joy; at Your right hand are pleasures forevermore."

The valley can be dark, the valley can be scary, and the valley can be lonely, but in the valley, you can meet face-to-face with God. That is what it's all about.

11

DRY BONES

As I'm getting older, I'm realizing more and more that movies just aren't the same as they used to be. Don't get me wrong, I love watching movies. I like all kinds of movies—comedy, romance, rom-com, suspense, intense. I pretty much like all movies except scary ones. Now before you start judging me and saying I'm a scaredy-cat or anything like that, it's not the scary I don't enjoy. A good jumpy-jump in a movie once in a while is entertaining to me. It's just the fact that 99.9 percent of all scary movies have TERRIBLE story lines and less-than-fulfilling endings. They never end well, ESPECIALLY zombie movies. Ugh, don't even get me started on zombie movies. Why can't they ever conclude well? Why is it that all these zombie movies leave it open-ended? Have you noticed that? There's rarely a cure or even an explanation as to what caused the zombies in the first place. The characters, the ones that survive at least, just start living their new lives in colonies somewhere in the middle of the woods, neglecting the reality that the zombie issue is still a thing. A good movie comes around once in a good while, but let's just talk about the movies from the nineties for a bit. Movies in the eighties and nineties are classics. Movies nowadays are, a lot of the time, remakes of movies from the nineties. For example, have you seen the new *Lion King* movie? By new, I mean remade, computer-animated version? It's really good if I do say so myself. *Lion King* is a movie that's very, VERY near to my heart. When I was a little kid, I would watch *Lion King* over and over again. No movie makes me cry like *Lion King* does. Don't judge me. If you don't cry in *Lion King* when Mufasa dies, I'm convinced that you don't have a heart. There's a part in the movie where Simba and Nala, when they were little cubs, went adventuring to a place they were warned not to go to, the elephant graveyard. That place is nasty-looking. Simba and Nala roll up on this place, and they see a desolate, deserted landscape that's decorated with elephant bones. When I see this part of the movie, I can't help but think of the next Bible story we will look at in learning about the valley.

This part of scripture is actually titled the Valley of Dry Bones. It's a prophetic vision that was given to a guy named Ezekiel, who was a priest that had lived in Jerusalem during the first Babylonian attack. Though the city wasn't completely destroyed, Babylon took some Israelites as captives and brought them into exile. Ezekiel was among those who were taken as prisoners. The exile in Babylon was a significant portion of what we discussed in the last chapter regarding going through fire. During the exile, God spoke to His people through prophets to not only bring truth and clarity as to why everything was happening the way it was but to offer a sense of hope for the days to come. This particular vision that God gave to Ezekiel is super unique and extremely applicable to us today. Let's take a journey through the valley of dry bones:

> The Lord took hold of me, and I was carried away by the Spirit of the Lord to a valley filled with bones. He led me all around among the bones that covered the valley floor. They were scattered everywhere across the ground and were completely dried out. Then He asked me, "Son of man, can these bones become living people again?" "O Sovereign Lord," I replied, "You alone know the answer to that." Then He said to me, "Speak a prophetic message to these bones and say, 'Dry bones, listen to the word of the Lord! This is what the Sovereign Lord says:

Look! I am going to put breath into you and make you live again! I will put flesh and muscles on you and cover you with skin. I will put breath into you, and you will come to life. Then you will know that I am the Lord.'" So I spoke this message, just as He told me. Suddenly as I spoke, there was a rattling noise all across the valley. The bones of each body came together and attached themselves as complete skeletons. Then as I watched, muscles and flesh formed over the bones. Then skin formed to cover their bodies, but they still had no breath in them. Then He said to me, "Speak a prophetic message to the winds, son of man. Speak a prophetic message and say, 'This is what the Sovereign Lord says: Come, O breath, from the four winds! Breathe into these dead bodies so they may live again.'" So, I spoke the message as He commanded me, and breath came into their bodies. They all came to life and stood up on their feet...a great army." (Ezekiel 37:1–10)

God will lead you TO and THROUGH some seemingly impossible valleys in life. What we do in the valley will determine how we are on the other side of it. God let Ezekiel into a vision of a valley. While Ezekiel was in this valley, the Lord told him to do three things: acknowledge what he saw, determine what he believed, and begin to speak into existence things that didn't exist yet. These three things are key for us to make it through our valleys.

The first question that God asked Ezekiel when they were in the valley was "What do you see?" The vision opens up with a description of what Ezekiel saw in the valley. He describes bones that were completely dry and scattered across the floor of the valley. Acknowledging what you see in the valley is EXTREMELY important if you want to begin to heal in the valley. We are so good at ignoring the pain we feel. Our culture is professional at developing things to distract us from what's actually going on inside our hearts. So many of us are in a valley right now, and because of our fear of feelings, we deflect and find anything that will make us numb. *Feel* is the four letter word that trips a lot of people up. What is it about feelings that is so intimidating? For me, when I feel things, it means that I'm vulnerable. Vulnerability is something that is extremely uncomfortable because it exposes the real you. For many of us, we don't like the real us, so vulnerability is avoided at all costs. To actually see what's in your valley requires intentionality and humility.

When we make the decision to stop and see what bones are in our valley, we might be exposed to and made aware of what stage of grief we find ourselves in. Grief is something that is natural and necessary after any storm or fire. The longer you wait to feel and go through the grieving process, the longer you will find yourself in the valley. Grief is simply our response to loss. In order to go through loss, you must allow yourself to not only grieve but to grieve properly and intentionally. According to scientific research, there are five stages of grief: denial and isolation, anger, bargaining, depression, and acceptance. People who are grieving don't necessarily go through the stages in the same order or experience all of them. Ultimately, the goal of grieving is to accept and go through loss. Keep in mind that everyone grieves differently. Some people will wear their emotions on their sleeve and be outwardly emotional, while others experience grief internally and not shed a tear at all. The first reaction to learning about our valley is to deny and isolate. This avoids the healing process because, subconsciously, healing means hurting. There was a time that I sprained my ankle really bad. It's not an epic story at all. I wish it were, but in all honesty, it's kind of embarrassing. When I was an intern, part of our weekly schedule was a time of working out. Working out is definitely not on my list of enjoyable things, but hey, I get it. Healthy and disciplined bodies can translate to a healthy and disciplined spiritual life. Sure thing. Anyways, there was a workout day where all of us interns went to a park that was down the street to play some capture the flag. There were fourteen interns, so it was easy to split into two teams. Capture the flag is a relatively low-impact activity, but for some reason, whenever I play it, I get seriously injured. This particular match lasted roughly thirty minutes. I went hard the whole time, diving, dipping, ducking, and dodging. It was intense. When the individual that oversaw the activities gave the five-minute warning, it was over. Our team was up by multiple scores, and the other team had no chance at catching up. I was guarding one of the faster guys on the other team. We were pacing back and forth. I was watching like a hawk on some prey. When he flinched, I was ready to pounce. As the whistle blew to signal the end of the match, we shook hands and began walking back to where we would all gather to do some post-game stretches. As I was walking back, I stepped in a very slight ditch, which caused my ankle to roll. I felt a pop and instantly started getting light-headed. I sat down because I felt like I was going to pass out. You know that feeling of tunnel vision you get when you stand up too fast? Yeah, it was that, except it wasn't going away. I laid down on the grass, and as soon as everyone congregated around me, I sat up and threw up everything that was in my stomach. After that, I knew I wasn't going to die, so I got some water, and we saddled up to go back to the church. When we finally got back, I rolled up my pant leg just to see my ankle, which was literally the size of a baseball. It was HUGE and purple. It looked nasty but didn't hurt that bad. The next day, the swelling went down, and it started to HURT. Pain, in this particular situation, meant that the healing process began. Many of us are still walking around numb and swollen from a break, in denial of the potential to heal. It hurts to heal. Denial and isolation buffer the immediate shock of a loss and can potentially numb us to our emotions. One who is in denial blocks out words and hides from facts. Isolation can also cause us to start believing that life is meaningless and that nothing is of any value anymore. Anger is another aspect to grief. When we lose someone or something and we begin to feel the pain from that, anger is a way to let out sadness or aggression. Bargaining is another normal reaction to grief. Bargaining can be summed up with "if only" statements. "If only we had gone to the doctor sooner. If only I was there with them." The underlying feeling that accompanies bargaining is guilt. We start to place the blame for whatever happened on ourselves because we believe that we could have done something to prevent it. This too is a normal response to grief. Depression is something that hits some people harder than others. This was actually the stage in the grief cycle that I found myself in. I didn't bargain. I didn't isolate. I wasn't angry. But I found myself depressed. I wasn't motivated to get up and do anything. I didn't enjoy living my life anymore. I would have much rather stayed in my bed all day. I was stuck in this never-ending cycle, until I finally learned that I was grieving. Being made aware of the grieving process helps people who are in the valley realize they are in the valley. Once you realize you're in the valley, you can start to heal. What do you see right now? Are there some things in your life that you have decided to sweep under the rug because they are too painful to look at? Have you heard the line "seeing is believing?" This couldn't be a truer statement. When we allow God to open our eyes to see the truth as to what is happening, that truth sets us free. God sees all things in our life and still continues to love us unconditionally. Let that one sink in!

After God had Ezekiel see and acknowledge the valley he was in, the next step in the valley process was believing. God asks Ezekiel, "Do you believe these bones can live again?" This step is all about faith. Once you see and acknowledge the actual situation you're in, it's time to add in faith. Having a relationship with Jesus gives you the ability to add this step. In the world, the equation goes like this: you + your circumstance = feelings. The equation with Jesus in the mix goes a little something like this: you + your circumstance + what you believe = feelings. Life with Jesus unlocks a whole new dimension to going through the valley. We aren't limited only to what we see. There is a whole realm of things unseen still yet to be discovered. In 2 Corinthians 5:7, it says, "For we live by believing and not by seeing." With Jesus, we don't need to see it to believe it. Faith is everything in our relationship with God. No matter how hopeless your situation may seem, you can still have faith. Even if you feel as though Jesus is being silent, that doesn't mean He isn't listening, and that definitely doesn't mean stop having faith. In Matthew 15, there's a story of a woman that never gives up asking Jesus for a miracle.

> A Gentile woman who lived there came to Him, pleading, "Have mercy on me, O Lord, Son of David! For my daughter is possessed by a demon that torments her severely." But Jesus gave her no reply, not even a word. Then His disciples urged Him to send her away. "Tell her to go away," they said. "She is bothering us with all her begging." "Dear woman," Jesus said to her, "your faith is great. Your request is granted." And her daughter was instantly healed. (Matthew 15:22–23, 28)

Don't ever limit God. In your current situation, once you've been able to acknowledge the reality of it, what are you now believing for? Our belief is the driving force behind our feelings.

Once Ezekiel saw the valley and started to believe for a miracle, he began to speak. "Speak a prophetic message to these bones…"

I challenge you today. In the areas that you see death in your life, speak life. If you knew how much power was in your words, you would never let yourself speak negatively again. If you see darkness, speak light. If you see brokenness, speak wholeness. If you see hopelessness, speak hope. If you see death, SPEAK LIFE.

> Death and life are in the power of the tongue, and those who love it will eat its fruits. (Proverbs 18:21)

Speaking death comes so easily to people. It's like whenever something challenging happens, our natural response is to speak death over it. Why not retrain your brain to operate in faith? Why not dare to dream again? Today, what is your faith confession? There is so much power in a prophetic declaration. See how much power God has in His words? He merely spoke, and the universe was created. He has put His very breath into us with the same authority through Jesus. My question to you today is how are you using your authority? If your parents keep on fighting, rather than complaining about it and confessing that it will never change, speak life over it. Say something like, "I believe that my parents will begin to reconcile. I speak peace over my home in Jesus's name." If you're having a hard time finding a job, rather than getting discouraged because the doors are closing, start to declare new doors opening in Jesus's name. There is BREAKTHROUGH in your faith confessions. In the valley, in order to heal and be restored, ask yourself, what do I see, what do I believe, and what now will I speak?

12

THE OTHER SIDE

I am completely confident in the reality of God's timing. Though at times it feels like He's running a bit late, when looking at life in reverse, God is always present and always on time. This final chapter of the book doesn't get any more real than it's about to get. After Karen and I lost Asher, it was an extremely challenging season. Extremely challenging is a severe understatement. I searched for just about every logical reason out there in an attempt to assign purpose to why my boy didn't make it. No matter how hard I tried, no matter how far I searched, nothing ever sufficed. There are times in life when terrible things happen, and there's no explanation as to why. This is a hard reality to accept, but it's true. It's human nature to try and explain things that happen, to blame someone, even if that someone is ourselves. Before going through what Karen and I went through, I was honestly a professional at avoiding pain. I knew all the subconscious tricks in the book. I could dodge tears like a professional. It wasn't until we were placed into a situation that was so heartbreaking that I was faced with a choice, to give up or go through it. It's not in my nature to give up, so I began this journey of going through it. That verse, our key verse in Isaiah 43, was the first thing that penetrated my fragile heart in the valley. It was that verse that again opened up my heart to God. It was that verse that took me on this adventure of discovering the different things that we as humans go through. It was mind-blowing to realize how many people have

163

lost a baby. People that I've known for years and have never known that they went through a similar thing that Karen and I did. Though whenever someone loses a baby, it's not always at the same time in the developmental process. Loss is loss, and tragedy is tragedy, no matter when it comes. I was overwhelmed by the amount of support that Karen and I received when this happened. The people around us really rallied together to show us love and care. In the valley, when I finally decided to move past my bitterness, the Lord started to give birth to a vision to write a book. A book that was going to be used all over the world to bring a sense of comfort to individuals who find themselves in a season that seems impossible. A book that was to be a beacon of light to those who felt trapped in darkness. Beginning to write this book was a very painful decision because it meant reliving a lot of what Karen and I went through. I'm not really sure how long most books take to write, though I'm assuming some are faster than others, but this book in particular took about a year and a half. I started writing this while I was still in the middle of going through the pain. In all honesty, it was rather therapeutic to get my thoughts out onto a computer screen. This book isn't a compilation of things that I've studied and read about academically. It's a collection of tools that I discovered along the way while going through each of those particular elements. Even in the midst of writing everything down, there were moments when I had to pause and really challenge the thought of if I truly believe what it is I'm writing. Even so, I continued forward one step at a time. It was a couple months after we lost Asher that Karen, and I felt a release to start trying to get pregnant again. We heard stories of people who lost their baby and then a couple months later got pregnant again with their son or daughter that they have now. If their first baby didn't pass away, they wouldn't have the child that they have now. This was a thought that I started to cling to. I never wanted to replace Asher, but I knew that if Karen and I could get pregnant shortly after we lost him, it would assign some sort of meaning to the pain. Month after month passed by and nothing. Whenever I had the thought "Surely, this is the month," it always ended with a negative pregnancy test. Social media is a dangerous thing when you're in this place. I started to scroll and see everyone around us getting pregnant. It seemed like everyone who was married and near our age either had kids already or was getting pregnant. Each month developed more and more sadness in my heart. There were times when I questioned God's existence, if I'm allowed to say that. There were times, with tears streaming down my face, when I would yell at Him and say things like, "Do you even care? Why would you let us get pregnant once and then not let us get pregnant again?" Let me just say that I'm so thankful for God's patience with us. All throughout this process, I kept a journal. In this journal are words that poured straight from my heart. Words of discouragement, fear, doubt, and sometimes, a glimmer of hope. The moment I took my eyes off of myself for a second, I started to grow faith again. There were, for sure, moments that my faith was just an ember sitting at the bottom of a pile of twigs. Faith that was once a fire for God was now barely holding on. There were brief moments when the wind would pick up and the embers would spark a bit, causing me to write things in faith and hope. There were also moments that I was really fighting. I want to take a moment to share with you one of my journal entries from 2020 to give you a glimpse into the psalms of my life:

January 11, 2020

I sit here this morning, not mad, but definitely a little confused and frustrated. Just found out AGAIN that Karen and I aren't pregnant. I have so many unanswered questions that I've needed to learn to live with. In a year that I believe You will restore me, how will my faith be restored if every month around this time it gets shattered? In the depth of my soul I trust You, Lord. I know there will be a morning this year that I will start an entry with, "It finally happened..." I just don't know when that day will come. Help me, Father, to delight myself in You. For I know that when I do that, You promise that You grant us the desires

of our hearts. Father, You've given me so much...
Help me, by the power of Your spirit within me
to discover a deep contentment. Help my eyes,
physically and spiritually, to be fixated on You.
May they not deviate and fall into comparison.
The story You've written for me and Karen is
unique and very beautiful. Even through this
wrestle, I know You are restoring me.

This entry was, admittingly so, one of the more faith-filled
entries. There were some that were so real in acknowledging the hurt
that I was processing through. There were moments of doubt, fear,
frustration, faith, hope, thankfulness. If you were given the opportunity to read all my journals, you'd be convinced that it was a script
for a soap opera on daytime television.

There are moments in life that I really can't deny God's reality and involvement in our lives. Moments like meeting Karen, getting into my internship, and beginning my career as a youth pastor. Looking back, it makes NO sense, outside of it involving God's
hand at work. This book is another one of those "only God" things.
This morning, exactly a year and a half from the day that we lost
Asher, Karen and I found out that we are pregnant. This is happening right now and unfolding as I write these words down. You can
look at something like this and call it coincidence, but I choose to
believe that God's timing is well at work. After more than a year of
questioning and worrying and struggling with faith, our prayer has
finally been answered. The day the last chapter of this book is written is the day we learn about being pregnant. Is it to say that God
waited until I finished this book to let us get pregnant? No, of course
not. It doesn't work like that. But what I am saying, with clarity
of mind and heart, is that God wanted to make a clear concluding
point to not only this book but for you, my friend, who are reading
this right now. You may feel that the season you're walking through
could break you. It won't. You may be discouraged with the thought
of God not caring about the desires of your heart, but He does. You
may think that God has forgotten you, but He hasn't. In fact, you are

His masterpiece. My prayer is that my life, through the good and bad days, is a trophy of God's grace. When people see me, I don't want them to see a person who has made accomplishments in his own strength. I want them to see Jesus. Friend, I genuinely pray that this book encouraged you. I pray that you gain a new sense of purpose in the pain. I pray that you begin to believe that you're not alone. I pray that you see God's love and care for you rather than blaming Him for the bad things that happen. I pray that instead of ignoring the hurts in your life, you boldly begin to face them. Friend, there will be a day that you step out on the other side. There will be a day that you look back and say "Remember when…" You are more than a conqueror. Your story is being written as you read these words. The storm will never take you out. The fire will never burn you up. The valley will never drive you to despair. You WILL make it THROUGH.

ABOUT THE AUTHOR

Brandon Maurizio is the youth pastor of Crosspoint Church in Santa Clarita, California. He has been serving in youth ministry collectively for over ten years and has had the opportunity to travel to multiple states and countries to speak at churches and other meetings. He takes pleasure in simple things like drinking black coffee, wearing flannels in the fall time, Nike shoes, and playing Clash Royale. He and his wife, Karen, have two chiweenie fur babies, Dallas and Peanut, a baby on the way, and a son, Asher, who is in heaven.

TIA information can be obtained
w.ICGtesting.com
in the USA
0012240621

9 781098 076085